Reindeer Days Remembered

This book is dedicated to the
reindeer herders and their families.

Elisa J. Hart with the assistance
of Inuvialuit Co-researchers

Reindeer Days Remembered
Researched and written by Elisa J. Hart

Assistant researchers:
Laura Ettagiak Orchard
Charles Komeak
Naudia Lennie

Interpreter/researchers:
Agnes Gruben White
Lena Anikina
Lillian Elias
Agnes Felix
Noah Felix

Graphic design team:
Elisa and Jill Hart
Page Layout:
Jill Hart

Copy editing:
Luisa Alexander Izzo

This project was funded in part by the Northern Oil and Gas Action Plan, the Inuvialuit Cultural Resource Centre, and the Prince of Wales Northern Heritage Centre (Department of Education, Culture and Employment, GNWT).

PRINCE OF WALES
NORTHERN
HERITAGE
CENTRE

Logistical support was provided by the Polar Continental Shelf Project (PCSP) and the Aurora Research Institute. Polar Continental Shelf Project Report No. 00999.

© Inuvialuit Cultural Resource Centre, 2001
ISBN 0-9683636-7-9

Keywords: Reindeer, Canada, oral history, Inuvialuit, Inupiat, Inuit, Gwich'in, Saami, Laplander, Mackenzie Delta

Inuvialuit Cultural Resource Centre
Box 2120
Inuvik, NT X0E 0T0

Inuvialuit Cultural Resource Centre

Photo Credits:
Front Cover:
Ellen Binder, Donald Pingo (behind), Joseph Avik, Mary Avik, and Jimmy Komeak at Reindeer Station, July 1992. (Elisa Hart)

Reindeer hitched to sleds. (Based on photo by A.L. Fleming/NWT Archives/N-1979-050-0309)

Back Cover:
The view from the sled. (Based on photo by A.L. Fleming /NWT Archives/N-1979-050-0314)

Watermark:
A herd at roundup stands quietly in a corral, August 1955. (Based on photo by D. Wilkinson/NWT Archives/N-1979-051-1143)

Printed in Canada by Friesens
First published in 2001

Contents

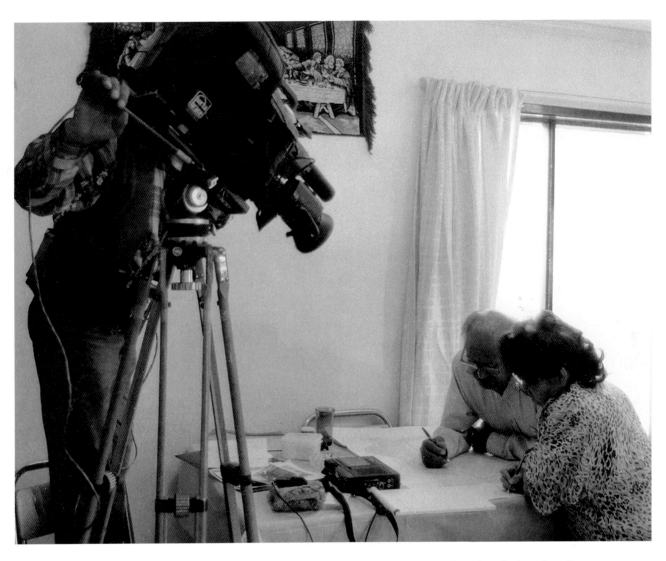

Agnes Gruben White and Danny Sydney locate places associated with reindeer herding on a map. Tom Smith of the Inuvialuit Communications Society videotapes them for the program *Tamapta*. (Elisa Hart)

Preface

This book is based on interviews with former reindeer herders and their family members in the early 1990s. The project was supported by the Northern Oil and Gas Action Program (NOGAP) and conducted by the Prince of Wales Northern Heritage Centre in Yellowknife. NOGAP funded projects that assessed the potential impacts of hydrocarbon development in the Beaufort/Delta Region. This project focused on making an inventory of Inuvialuit heritage sites.[1] Some of the places identified were the locations of old reindeer corrals and camps. In 1991, we interviewed elders in Tuktoyaktuk to learn more about the use of these places and about their experiences in the early days of the reindeer industry, when the federal government controlled it. In 1992, we also interviewed elders from Inuvik. One more interview was done in 2001.

We interviewed most elders in their homes, and some on day trips to places associated with the reindeer industry. One day trip was to Warren Point, to see the remains of a corral that had once belonged to Joseph Avik and Bob Panaktalok. As Reindeer Station played a key role in the history of reindeer herding, we made two day trips there with elders from Inuvik and Tuktoyaktuk.

Recommendations from the elders and the interpreter/researchers helped us decide whom to interview. Our thanks to those who participated in this project:

Rhoda Allen	Ned Kayotuk
Eva Apsimik	Jimmy Komeak
William Apsimik	Edgar Kotokak
Joseph Avik	Nellie Lester
Mary Avik	Raymond Mangelana
Ellen Binder	Donald Pingo
Otto Binder	David Roland
Adam Emaghok	Olga Roland
Annie Emaghok	Peter Rufus
Jimmy Gordon	Madeline Smith
Laura Kangegana	Danny Sydney

Researchers Elisa Hart and Charles Komeak, with Mathew Anikina (child) on a trip to record heritage sites, 1993. (Ken Anikina)

Laura Ettagiak Orchard (left) of the research team, with Mary Avik outside the remains of the Aviks' corral at Igluk, near Warren Point, 1991. (Elisa Hart)

The Research Team

A number of people participated in the project as part of the research team. Laura Ettagiak Orchard and Charles Komeak of Tuktoyaktuk and Naudia Lennie of Inuvik assisted with interviews and transcribed interview tapes.

Our interpreters were Agnes Gruben White, Lena Anikina, and Noah and Agnes Felix in Tuktoyaktuk, and Lillian Elias in Inuvik. The interpreters were also researchers. They asked some questions of their own, verified information, and recommended people to be interviewed. My sincere thanks go to all those who worked on the project.

The Inuvialuit Communications Society accompanied us on our trips to Reindeer Station and produced a video on the elders' experience for their weekly program *Tamapta*.

For Whom is This Book Written?

This book is written for a number of audiences. It is meant for the elders and their families who took part in the reindeer industry. We hope that elders may use it to explain their experiences to their children or grandchildren. We tried to make it very visual in format to facilitate such discussions.

The book is also meant as an overview of the reindeer industry that can be used in high school classes on local history and geography. Teachers can expand on the topics of interest to them. Elders or other experts on topics touched on in the book could be invited into the classroom to provide their knowledge and perspectives. We also hope that the book will be of interest to the general public.

The Focus of the Book

The history of the reindeer industry in the Beaufort/Mackenzie Region is very complex. Among the many different people and agencies involved were government employees, Inuvialuit, Inupiat from Alaska, trainees from the Kitikmeot Region of the Central Arctic, a small number of Gwich'in, and Saami from Norway. This book is not meant to reflect all of their views. It is meant to provide insights into the experience of Inuvialuit reindeer herders in the early days of the reindeer industry. It also provides glimpses into the experience of herders' families. It focuses on the time when herders, on skis or on foot, kept a constant watch over the herds, from 1935 to approximately 1964. Background information was gathered through research of archival and published documents. More research is needed to document other aspects of the industry in more detail than is presented here.

Plain Language and End Notes

Since I hope that this book will be used in high schools, I have tried to make the language easy to read. To avoid breaking up the flow of the text, I placed references in notes at the end. These notes provide

Agnes Gruben White was an interpreter/researcher for the project. (John Poirier)

Agnes and Noah Felix were interpreter/researchers for the project. (Dennis Felix)

7

additional information for people interested in learning more about the reindeer industry.

Interview Tapes and Quotes

Quotations from interviews with elders appear throughout the text. The year of the recording and the interview tape number are given after each quote. The tapes will soon be turned over to the Northwest Territories Archives (NWT Archives) in Yellowknife.

Anyone who has ever seen an unedited transcript of his or her own conversation notices that it does not read smoothly. In speaking, we often "hum" and "ha," backtrack on a thought, or change subject in mid-sentence. The quotations have been edited to remove these "bumps," and sometimes words in square brackets have been added to clarify meaning. The symbol (…) is used to show that part of a response or an interviewer's question has been omitted.

Project Support

Several organizations supported this project. As mentioned above, the Northern Oil and Gas Action Program provided funding to the Prince of Wales Northern Heritage Centre to conduct the initial research.

Going home from a day trip to Reindeer Station by helicopter. Joseph Avik and Donald Pingo with Jimmy Komeak in the back, July 1992. (Elisa Hart)

Naudia Lennie was a member of the research team. She is standing in front of a photo display of her family tree that she researched and produced while working at the Prince of Wales Northern Heritage Centre in Yellowknife. (Elisa Hart)

The Polar Continental Shelf Project (PCSP) gave logistical support, which included helicopter time for some day trips as well as meals and housing for project staff at the PCSP base in Tuktoyaktuk. We thank PCSP, and particularly the staff of the Tuktoyaktuk base camp: Claude Brunet, Gerry McEachern, Debbie Clouthier, and Eric Osmond. The Inuvik Research Centre (now the Aurora Research Institute) also provided accommodation in the summer of 1992. We also thank the helicopter pilots we worked with, particularly the late David Nasogaluak, Jr., and Ray Anderson. They were very attentive to the elders and helped make the project a success.

Larry Gordon, Director of Community Development, Inuvialuit Regional Corporation (IRC), provided funding for the project. Pat Winfield, Coordinator of the Inuvialuit Cultural Resource Centre, IRC, provided funding for layout design, copy editing, and printing this book.

Photographs

The photographs shown come from a variety of places. Most are from the National Archives of Canada in Ottawa or the Northwest Territories Archives in Yellowknife. The photographer, the name of the archive, and the accession number are provided for each photograph so that readers can order copies.

National Archives of Canada
395 Wellington Street
Ottawa, Ontario
K1A 0N3

NWT Archives
Box 1320
Yellowknife, NT
X0E 1C0

Other photographs were taken during the project or were provided by individuals or organizations. The photographers or those providing photographs are credited

Lena Anikina was an interpreter/researcher for the project. (John Poirier)

Many Thanks

Others not already mentioned deserve thanks for their assistance and support. Charles Arnold, Director of the Prince of Wales Northern Heritage Centre (PWNHC), made the project possible. John Poirier of PWNHC scanned many of the images and provided training in photography to some project staff.

John Nagy of Resources, Wildlife and Economic Development (RWED), Government of the Northwest Territories (GNWT), Inuvik, kindly provided photographs of grazing areas and caribou. John Cournoyea, also of RWED, provided photographs of a grizzly bear and a lynx.

Many thanks to Lloyd Binder, Dick Hill, Renie Arey, Charles Komeak, Nellie Cournoyea, Peter Silaotsiak, Charles Arnold, and Pat Winfield, who reviewed a draft of the book. I appreciate the hard work and artistic skill of Jill Hart, who did the page layout, map and charts. It was fun working together as a team on the design. And finally, it was tremendously comforting to have Luisa Alexander Izzo as the copy editor.

after the photograph caption. Thanks to the many people who provided photographs, and to those who helped identify people in photographs. Thanks to people in other communities who helped scan photographs of elders for us. These include the staff of the Nunavut Planning Commission office in Cambridge Bay (Ikaluktutiak), and Frank Smith. Thanks also to Peggy Jay of the Inuvialuit Regional Corporation and Karen LeGresley Hamre of Yellowknife.

Lillian Elias with her parents, George and Martha Harry, 1992. (Elisa Hart)

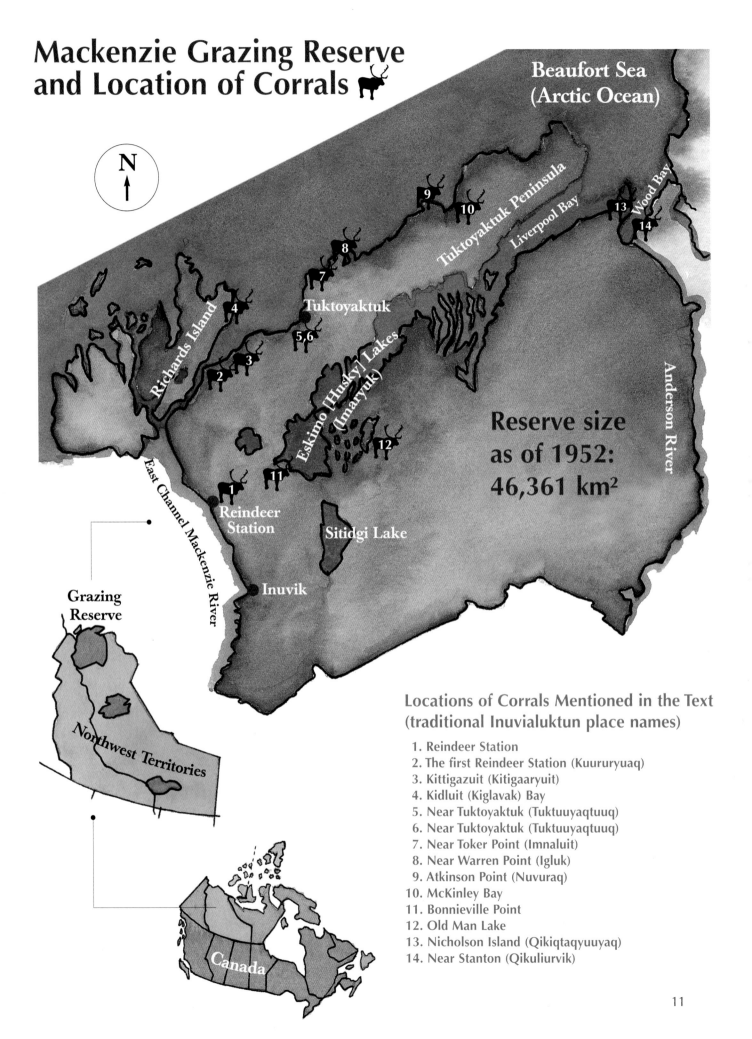

Mackenzie Grazing Reserve and Location of Corrals

Beaufort Sea (Arctic Ocean)

N

Tuktoyaktuk Peninsula

Liverpool Bay

Wood Bay

Richards Island

Tuktoyaktuk

Eskimo [Husky] Lakes (Imaryuk)

Anderson River

Reserve size as of 1952: 46,361 km²

East Channel Mackenzie River

Reindeer Station

Sitidgi Lake

Inuvik

Grazing Reserve

Northwest Territories

Canada

Locations of Corrals Mentioned in the Text (traditional Inuvialuktun place names)

1. Reindeer Station
2. The first Reindeer Station (Kuururyuaq)
3. Kittigazuit (Kitigaaryuit)
4. Kidluit (Kiglavak) Bay
5. Near Tuktoyaktuk (Tuktuuyaqtuuq)
6. Near Tuktoyaktuk (Tuktuuyaqtuuq)
7. Near Toker Point (Imnaluit)
8. Near Warren Point (Igluk)
9. Atkinson Point (Nuvuraq)
10. McKinley Bay
11. Bonnieville Point
12. Old Man Lake
13. Nicholson Island (Qikiqtaqyuuyaq)
14. Near Stanton (Qikuliurvik)

11

Introduction

"When I was 15 years old...I started learning everything [about] the herding life when I reached Reindeer Station. How to ski, drive reindeer, and all that moving around. There was only manpower in those days, no skidoos, no planes whatsoever. We used to ski or use a team of reindeer, and in the summer when there was no snow you just walked to follow the reindeer. That was a 24-hour job in those days."

Jimmy Komeak (1991, Tape 9)

Working in the reindeer industry during the early years, before snowmobiles, was a memorable experience. Some former herders recall it as a hard yet enjoyable life; others remember it as just plain difficult. This book provides the perspective of reindeer herders and their wives who were part of the Mackenzie reindeer operation from the 1930s to the early 1960s. This was a time when herding was done on foot or on skis under difficult conditions. The "insider's view" is presented through quotations from oral history interviews with elders. Their memories and personal views are the heart of this story. We also used archival documents and publications to learn how and why the government made some of its decisions regarding the reindeer industry.

Jimmy Komeak, Tuktoyaktuk, 1995. (John Poirier)

A herd at roundup stands quietly in a corral, August 1955. (Based on photo by D. Wilkinson/NWT Archives/ N-1979-051-1143)

During this 30-year period, approximately 70 men received training as herders, and some went on to manage their own herds.[2] These men were from different areas: some were local Inuvialuit, a few were Gwich'in, others were Inupiat from various parts of Alaska and Inuit from the Coronation Gulf area of the Central Arctic.

The story of the reindeer industry presented here is historical. However, the industry is still in operation as an Inuvialuit-owned company. The book also gives a brief overview of the industry since 1964, up to the most recent developments in herd ownership.

Reindeer for the Delta

Mangilaluk. Elders refer to him as the first chief of Tuktoyaktuk. (Courtesy of Mangilaluk School)

"The way I heard it right from the beginning, old Mangilaluk was the chief, so [the government] asked him if it was okay to bring the herd down here so they could use them for meat. That was pretty good because there were no caribou around at that time."

Peter Rufus (1991, Tape 20)

Peter Rufus, 1991. Peter was a reindeer herder longer than anyone else. (Elisa Hart)

"The caribou migration stopped coming to the west. This was the reason they brought the herd from Alaska. For some unexplainable reason the caribou quit migrating, and there was a real need for meat. Sixty years later, the caribou came back. You can't control caribou movements: they're not domesticated. You can control reindeer—they're semi-domesticated..."

Ellen Binder (1992, Tape 10)

Ellen Binder, 1965. (Dick Hill)

Government representatives had approached Chief Mangilaluk about signing a treaty. Mangilaluk, after meeting with Bob Cockney (Nuligak) and other advisors, told the government that they did not want to sign a treaty. He said that rather than offer a $5 treaty payment, the government could provide something useful, like reindeer for the people to eat.[3] Eventually, reindeer were delivered to the eastern side of the Mackenzie Delta in 1935. The government wanted to start this industry for several reasons.

Dr. A.W. Wakefield and unidentified man with reindeer at St. Anthony, Labrador, 1909. (Based on photo by L. Learmonth/NWT Archives/N-1987-033-0002)

The caribou had disappeared from the Mackenzie Delta area. Caribou hunting had increased around the turn of the century to supply American whaling crews with meat. Caribou were often used to feed dog teams, which were more numerous at that time. These factors, along with a shift in caribou migration, had left few caribou in the area.[4] The government wanted to fill the gap by establishing a reindeer herding industry, so that reindeer could provide food and skins for local people. It was hoped that Inuvialuit would take up reindeer management as a way of supporting themselves. Herding was considered a more reliable occupation than trapping, given the ever-changing price of furs.

The government also thought that providing reindeer would relieve the pressure on other wildlife from hunting and trapping. If the reindeer industry proved successful in this region, the government planned to establish herds east to Baffin Island and south to Great Bear Lake.[5]

The government's plan was to hire apprentice herders who would learn enough about reindeer management to become herd owners. Once they were trained, the herders would be given reindeer from the government herd on loan to set up their own herds on separate grazing grounds. Once the new herds had increased, the herders would return to the government the same number of reindeer they had borrowed and keep the remaining animals. This process would continue until there were enough Native-owned herds that the government could stop being involved.

This was not the first time reindeer had been brought to Canada. Between 1908 and 1923, private organizations or the government had imported reindeer from Norway to Newfoundland, Quebec, and the Northwest Territories (around Fort Smith and on southern Baffin Island).[6] None of those attempts to start reindeer herds in Canada succeeded. For the next attempt at developing a reindeer industry, the government looked to Alaska for ideas.

They Came from Alaska

The reindeer herd on its way from Alaska. (Based on photo by R. Terpening/NWT Archives/N-1987-030-463)

Reindeer had been brought to Alaska from Siberia in 1892 and 1898, and the industry was booming.[7] Between 1926 and 1928, the Canadian government paid for a study of the land and vegetation along the Arctic Coast. Erling Porsild and his brother Robert (Bob) surveyed the territory from the Yukon/Alaska boundary, east to the Coppermine River, as well as the area just north of Great Bear Lake. They decided that the best place to bring reindeer was the Mackenzie Delta area.[8]

In 1929, the government signed a contract with the Lomen Reindeer Company of Alaska to deliver 3,442 reindeer to the Mackenzie Delta.[9] To drive the reindeer to Canada, the company hired Andrew Bahr, a respected Saami herder who was originally from Norway. The herd left Alaska in December 1929, on what was supposed to be a one-and-a-half to two-year journey.[10] It turned into a five-year struggle, full of hardships for both men and animals. Most of the original reindeer died along the way, but luckily enough calves were born to replace them. A number of articles and books have been written about this drive and the hardships experienced by both herders and reindeer.[11]

"They brought the herd over and they went back to Alaska. But the ones that married stayed here. Just Edwin [Allen]...[and] Mark Noksana stayed behind and married girls from around here."

Nellie Lester (1992, Tape 5)

Nellie Lester, Inuvik, 1992.
(Naudia Lennie)

Edwin and Rhoda Allen in the 1930s. Edwin came from Alaska with the reindeer herd. He met and married Rhoda and continued to live in the area. (Courtesy of Annie C. Gordon)

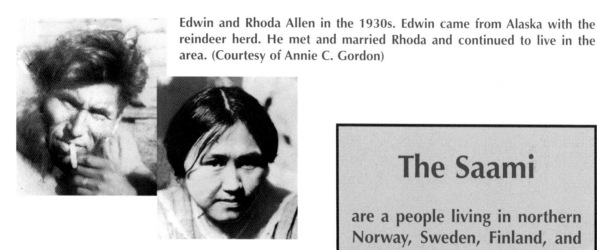

The Saami

are a people living in northern Norway, Sweden, Finland, and Russia. They are sometimes called Laplanders or Lapps, but *Saami* is the word they use for themselves. Because the Saami way of life has been closely linked to the reindeer for thousands of years, many Saami are expert reindeer herders.

Andrew Bahr hired Inupiat in Alaska to help with the drive. When the herd reached the Mackenzie Delta, not all of the Inupiat who started the drive wanted to return. Some men stayed behind and started families.

Andrew Bahr, the chief herder (on the left) and an unidentified man. (Based on photo by R. Terpening/NWT Archives/N-1987-030-467)

Christmas at the first Reindeer Station near Kuururyuaq. Back row: Asta Porsild, Susanna and baby Anna Tornensis, Anna and daughter Ellen Kristine Pulk, Inger and Berit Haetta. Front row: Louis Brockage, Isaac Pulk, Karin Porsild, and Nels Pulk, 1932. (Based on photo by A.E. Porsild/National Archives of Canada/PA-203205)

Getting Ready for the Reindeer

While the reindeer were being driven from Alaska, arrangements were being made for their arrival. The government brought three Saami herders from Norway, Mikkel Pulk, Matthis Haetta, and Aslak Tornensis, to help train apprentice herders. They would also train reindeer to pull sleds and train dogs to herd the reindeer.[12]

In 1930 and 1931, construction began for a corral and buildings in the Kittigazuit area.[13] This first reindeer station consisted of frame

"I knew Mikkel, Aslak, and Matthis...Two of them went back right away, as soon as they brought the herd here... but Mikkel stayed and became the chief herder... But we didn't understand them very well. When they talked, they talked their language...and they had to make signs sometimes."

David Roland (1992, Tape 53)

David and Olga Roland, Inuvik, 1992. (Elisa Hart)

The first Reindeer Station in 1931–1932. It was built at Kuururyuaq, although some called this area Kittigazuit (see box at right). Some herders referred to this as the "Old Station" once the new Reindeer Station was built further upriver. (Based on photo by A.E. Porsild/National Archives of Canada/PA-202533)

buildings and log houses. Some of those log houses are still standing today. Although people referred to the area as Kittigazuit, the station was located at a creek called Kuururyuaq.[14] This is the location that people in the area know as Army Camp, from the Loran navigation station that the Canadian and U.S. Air Forces built inland, behind the cabins, in the 1940s.

At some point later, the permanent Reindeer Station (or Reindeer Depot, as it was sometimes called) was built about 100 km further up the Mackenzie River. It was a much bigger camp, with buildings for staff housing, offices, and storage of various supplies and equipment. The location was considered good because it had firewood and ample supplies of the lichen that reindeer need to eat in winter.[15]

The Word *Kittigazuit*

is an English version of the Inuvialuktun name *Kitigaaryuit*. Kitigaaryuit is approximately 11 km east of Kuururyuaq. At one time, Kitigaaryuit was an important village and the central gathering place of the Kitigaaryumiut. In the 20th century, it was the location of a Hudson's Bay Company Post and Anglican mission. Now a National Historic Site, it is still used as a whaling camp.[16]

In 1933, the government also created the huge Mackenzie Reindeer Grazing Reserve, which covered 17,094 km^2.[17] This angered many local people, as they now needed a permit to hunt and trap on their traditional lands.

One of the remaining cabins at Kuururyuaq. (Elisa Hart)

The Reindeer Industry Begins

Reindeer arrive at the first Reindeer Station. (Based on photo by R. Terpening/NWT Archives/N-1987-030-0464)

On March 6, 1935, 2,370 reindeer were delivered to the first reindeer station at Kuururyuaq. At a cost of $65 each, the purchase price of the herd was $154,050.[18] The herders counted the animals and checked their condition. The fawns were a bit small from having been born and raised under such difficult circumstances. But the reindeer did well in their new grazing grounds, and in the first year about 800 new fawns were born.[19]

The government decided to use a method called "close" or "intensive" herding, which was based on the method used by the Saami. Close herding meant that the reindeer were not allowed to range freely. Herders stayed with the reindeer at all times to keep them together, within a few kilometres of each other.

In close herding, the herders had to keep up with the reindeer, and they used herd dogs to help them. The herders walked with the herd in summer and skied alongside the reindeer in winter. The deer were always on the move, eating as they went.

The close herding method was quite different from the "open" herding used in Alaska. There, herds were allowed to range together, and the herd owners would find out how many they had at the annual roundup of the animals. Close herding also meant moving the animals to specific grazing grounds throughout the year, rather than allowing them to wander.

"We had a hard time when we looked after the reindeer. You couldn't sleep long in the summer, and winter was the same. You had to make sure they didn't get away. We kept following the reindeer—walking... Twenty-four hours a day we kept taking turns watching the reindeer."
Edgar Kotokak (1991, Tape 25)

Edgar Kotokak, Tuktoyaktuk, 1993. Edgar started herding in the 1940s in the Anderson River area. (Charles Komeak)

The reindeer are finally in the corral near the first Reindeer Station at Kuururyuaq. (Based on photo by R. Terpening/NWT Archives/N-1987-030-466)

Finding Herders

Jimmy Komeak, Donald Pingo and Joseph Avik (Avingayoak) at Reindeer Station in 1992. Jimmy and Joseph were brought from the Cambridge Bay area. Donald is originally from Pt. Barrow, Alaska. (Ray Anderson)

The government had planned on training some boys from residential schools to become herders. Because of budget cuts, they decided to hire adult men instead.[20] However, not many Inuvialuit were interested in taking up the life of herders, as they were doing well as hunters and trappers. Over the years, men signed up as apprentice herders (or experienced men, as herders) for economic reasons.

"I needed some spending money...so I became a herder in 1942. The herders were the people in those days who did well. They learned how to hold on to a job, you know. Inuit are nomadic people...they didn't want to be tied down to a system that works by a clock. So [when] that system started coming, a lot of them learned through being reindeer herders. They had to stick to the time clock too. So that was a training period for nomadic people, actually."

Otto Binder (1992, Tape 52)

> "I could have been a herder when I was a young man, but when the fur was good, I didn't like to have a boss. Yes, then the fur [prices] got so low that I had to take a job. That was in 1953."
>
> David Roland (1992, Tape 53)

Early on in the reindeer operation, some trainees were brought from the Coronation Gulf area of the Central Arctic because the government planned on having reindeer in that area some day.[21] Trainees were also brought from the east, as few local men were attracted to herding, given their success in trapping. Some of these herders, such as Jimmy Komeak and his brother Joseph Avik, stayed on in the area. Others moved back east to communities such as Cambridge Bay (Ikaluktutiak) and Kugluktuk (formerly Coppermine). Some Inupiat from Alaska who were staying at places like Herschel Island were encouraged to try herding. Those herders who worked in the earliest days of the industry remember Joseph (Yaya) Sittichinli, a Gwich'in man who stayed with herding for some time.

Right: Billy Kikoak used to herd for Wallace Lucas and Peter Rufus, and for the main herd. (Courtesy of Maureen Pokiak)

Left: Kelly Ovayuak was one of the early reindeer herders who began when the herd was still in the Anderson River area. (Courtesy of Lena Anikina)

Jimmy and Jean Komeak with children Della and Charles at Aklavik, 1956. (Based on photo by E. Watt/NWT Archives/N-1990-005-0135)

Philip Raymond was one of the first reindeer herders in 1935. However, he enjoyed the life of a hunter and chose to do that instead. (Courtesy of Nellie Raymond)

The Herding Life

Charlie (Kitli) Rufus, 1930. (Based on photo by A.L. Fleming/NWT Archives/N-1979-050-0306)

The herding life was not an easy one. It was a mixture of hardship and sometimes isolation. The herders were tough individuals. They must have had incredible endurance to work the long hours and cover the ground that they did in those days, before there were ATVs or snowmobiles to help them.

"Sometimes we got tired. In the winter we went fast because we were on skis. When we walked in the summer...it was wet. Those creeks were hard to cross. I just took my clothes off, threw them across, and then swam across. In the summer, when the ice first melted, that's when [the water] was cold!"
Joseph Avik (1991, Tape 23)

Joseph Avik at Reindeer Station in July 1992. (Elisa Hart)

An apprentice's introduction to herding was an experience to remember. Apprentices learned on the job, and that was not always an easy beginning.

"The first time I went out herding, I never slept for 24 hours. On my way home, I was sleeping while walking. I thought to myself, 'This job is no good for me...I've got to look for another job.' I was 18 years old...I went to sleep for 12 hours or something like that. I wanted to quit...'I don't want to be out there.' I said to myself... Well anyway, I felt good the next day. [In a] couple of days I said, 'I'm ready to go again.' So, I went out again (laugh). [After] two or three times in my gear, I finally got used to it."

Jimmy Gordon (1992, Tape 4)

Jimmy Gordon of Inuvik holds up a reindeer collar that once belonged to Andrew Bahr. (Elisa Hart)

Herders taking a break. Joe Illasiak, Mikkel Pulk (far behind), Wallace Lucas (front), Peter Kaglik (with hat), and Roger Allen, 1940. (Based on photo by J.A. Parsons/National Archives of Canada/PA-101108)

Adam and Annie Emaghok, Tuktoyaktuk, 1993. Adam was both a herder and a herd manager. (Charles Komeak)

"Sometimes, especially in early fall, I think of a time I was at the Anderson River. We were camping out, me and Donald [Silaotsiak]. We just had a little piece of canvas to cover us up. After we slept for a few hours, when we got up, it was white all over [with snow]. But where we were [lying] it was just black. I think of that once in a while."

Adam Emaghok (2001, Tape 1)

Left: Helen and John Maksagak of Cambridge Bay in the early 1990s. John was a herder from the 1940s to the late 1950s. He first herded for Peter Kaglik in the Anderson River area and then for the main herd out of Reindeer Station. Later in life, Helen became the Commissioner of the Northwest Territories. (Courtesy of Helen Maksagak)

Right: Harry Amagonalok in the late 1990s. Harry was a herder in the Anderson River area for the main herd, and also herded for Joseph Avik and Bob Panaktalok. He now lives in Cambridge Bay (Ikaluktutiak). (Courtesy of Ann Kasook)

Herding was demanding work, especially when herders had to work the long, 24-hour shifts, or two-hour shifts throughout the night.

"We took turns on shift, and we never kept still. Someone always had to be with the herd. We had to take turns. We were always on the go."
Joseph Avik (1991, Tape 23)

The shift work depended on the time of year. During the fawning season, the herders kept a constant watch on the animals. If wolves were spotted, the men worked two-hour shifts through the night to protect the herd. This was very tiring work.

"You've got to watch [the herd] at night...You've got to go out every two hours...Somebody slept, somebody went out for two hours...even in 50 below, you had to stay out."
Ned Kayotuk (1992, Tape 55)

Ned Kayotuk, Inuvik, 1992. (Elisa Hart)

Below: Joseph (Yaya) Sittichinli, a Gwich'in herder, in 1937. Yaya Lake on Richards Island is named after him. (Based on photo by M. Meikle/ National Archives of Canada/PA-203208)

Right: Tom Aneroluk was a herder in the early 1940s who later returned to Cambridge Bay. (Courtesy of Ruth Wilcox)

Above: Temporary camp of herders on Richards Island, 1937. (Based on photo by M. Meikle/National Archives of Canada/PA-101721)

"If you used a tent, maybe some people would stay in it all the time, and the herd would stray away from you. We never used a sleeping bag in summertime: otherwise, if you slept too long, no more herd!"

Jimmy Komeak (1991, Tape 9)

Roger Kunuk in the mid-1960s. He was a herder for the main herd. (Courtesy of Annie Kunuk)

Sometimes the policies of the government made the herding life more difficult, or certainly less comfortable, than it might have been. In the fall, the herders were not allowed to use tents. As the cold weather set in and the vegetation started to die, the reindeer were always on the move looking for food, and the rut was on. It was too early in the season to use skis to keep up to them. Those in charge thought that if the herders got too comfortable in their tents, they might let the reindeer wander away.

Left: Joseph Pokiak, Tuktoyaktuk, 1993. Joseph was a herder for the main herd. (Charles Komeak)

Below: A. Erling Porsild with Matthis and Inger Haetta. The Haettas were one of the three Saami families brought from Norway by the Canadian government to train local people to become reindeer herders. (Based on photo by R.S. Finnie/ National Archives of Canada/PA-130424)

"When we first started, they didn't even allow us to have tents. In October, when the snow was coming, we had to stay outdoors: we were reindeer herding. [We'd] ski around, walk around, and build a campfire. One guy was up, one guy kept the fire going. No, [we] didn't even carry a sleeping bag."

Otto Binder (1992, Tape 52)

Otto Binder, Inuvik, 1992. (Elisa Hart)

The hardships of working in all kinds of weather throughout the year took a toll on most of the herders.

"I was going to quit and then the boss talked to me and said, 'You don't have to be a herder: you could be a labour foreman.' So I stayed and became a labour foreman...Work was pretty good. But the reason why I was going to quit the herding business [was] my legs. Boy! In the fall time, you had to stay out—no tent, snowing, raining...My legs started to get sore, so I was going to quit. And cold! Yes, that's why I have arthritis now."

David Roland (1992, Tape 53)

Raymond and Sarah Mangelana, Tuktoyaktuk, 1992. Raymond herded in the Anderson River area for Peter Kaglik. (Elisa Hart)

Mosquitoes!

In the early days of the reindeer industry, there was no bug repellent. The relentless mosquitoes made life difficult.

"Boy it was tough, no mosquito dope, nothing! We sat there on top of the hill...and made smoke. We really suffered at that time when we worked for the government."
Ned Kayotuk (1992, Tape 55)

Reindeer or caribou stand at the water's edge to get away from mosquitoes. Somewhere between Warren Point and Toker Point, 1991. (Elisa Hart)

Reindeer moving onto a sandy point of land to escape flies, Richards Island, 1937. (Based on photo by J.A. Parsons/ National Archives of Canada/PA-203207)

The mosquitoes tormented the reindeer as well, which in some ways made life easier for the herders:

"The [reindeer] moved quite a bit in June because of the mosquitoes...but never really separated. They were always in a bunch when mosquitoes came, and they constantly moved."

Donald Pingo (1992, Tape 9)

Donald Pingo, 1992. (Elisa Hart)

"In summertime it was good because the mosquitoes kept them together in a bunch. One time I got close to the reindeer and they were in a bunch in hot weather. There was a mad look about them. They were just black with mosquitoes! I should have had a camera. Then I could have taken a picture...it was just black!"

Peter Rufus (1991, Tape 20)

The Yearly Cycle of Activity

Reindeer crossing the East Channel of the Mackenzie River at Swimming Point, in their summer range, 1964. (Based on photo by S. Muller, Department of Information/NWT Archives/G-1979-023-1769)

There was a yearly cycle of activity, which involved moving the reindeer to new grazing grounds. Other annual events were a roundup of the reindeer in summer and a slaughter in late November to early December.

Keeping the herd on good grazing grounds throughout the year was important to the health of the animals. Herders had to make decisions about where to move the reindeer. Finding good grazing areas made life easier for the herders, as the reindeer would not need to wander off looking for food.

"We followed the ground that we thought was good for feeding. That way [the reindeer] didn't move much when you found a good feeding place. So we tried to hit the right place. If you hit the wrong place, they just kept walking. They knew it was no good. They wanted to eat, so they just kept going."

Peter Rufus (1991, Tape 20)

Moving the reindeer to new feeding areas also kept them from over-grazing the land.

Caribou feeding on upland tundra, the type of ground where reindeer graze in fall. (Courtesy of Resources, Wildlife and Economic Development, Inuvik Region, GNWT)

The yearly grazing cycle involved moving the reindeer about every three months. In spring, the herders moved the animals to fawning grounds. In summer, they needed to be where the coastal breezes would lessen the torment of the mosquitoes. In fall, they moved to areas that had both good grazing for the reindeer and wood for the herders.

In summer, reindeer eat various grasses and shrubs. In winter, they depend mostly on "reindeer moss," a type of lichen that scientists call *Cladonia rangiferina*. The reindeer eat other types of lichens too.

Left: "Reindeer moss," which is actually lichen, is the primary food of the reindeer in winter. (Courtesy of Resources, Wildlife and Economic Development, Inuvik Region, GNWT)

Caribou on the type of grazing ground used by reindeer in winter. This is where the "reindeer moss" or lichen grows. (Courtesy of Resources, Wildlife and Economic Development, Inuvik Region, GNWT)

Winter required moving to grounds where there was enough lichen for the reindeer to eat. Jimmy Komeak explains the movements of the main herd, which belonged to the government:

"In the old days, we moved the camp every three months...In the fall I started out from Kiglavak Bay[22] on Richards Island. We moved to the fall camp, and that's where we had to stay until after freeze-up. We stayed for three months... The bosses from Reindeer Station...took the women to Reindeer Station in a scow. The men were left behind.

After freeze-up, we teamed up our reindeer and moved to Reindeer Station. We stayed there for three months in fall. After killing and slaughtering [some] reindeer we moved inland, way back up behind Inuvik.

You know why we had to keep them moving? We wanted the reindeer to move onto fresh ground all the time, especially in winter. We stayed there for three months and then moved back to Reindeer Station in the spring...Before the ice got rotten, we moved to Kiglavak Bay on Richards Island...for summer for another three months."

Jimmy Komeak (1991, Tape 9)

The herders moved slowly from one grazing ground to another, so the reindeer could feed along the way. The distance from the summer to winter grounds varied, but some were about 120 km apart.

> "When the lakes got strong enough in fall, we started to bring [the reindeer] inland for winter. We didn't want to let them eat around here [the coast] because this is their feeding ground for summer. We never let them eat in the summer feeding place in winter. That's why we stayed inland all winter... We kept moving the deer to where they hadn't eaten."
>
> **Joseph Avik (1991, Tape 23)**

The areas where the main herd was kept changed over the years. Later, it was decided that the reindeer would cross from Richards Island to the fall grazing grounds before freeze-up. The result was quite an event to watch: several thousand reindeer would swim across the Mackenzie River together at a spot called Swimming Point. This crossing was also known as *Nalluq*, which means "to swim."

Mikkel Pulk, Chief Herder, and his dog Kobuk at the fawning grounds on Richards Islands, 1936. (Based on photo by J.A. Urquhart/National Archives of Canada/PA-121721)

Fawning Season

Linda Binder (holding a fawn) and Ellen Binder at a roundup at Swimming Point, June 2001. A close-up of the fawn, born late in the season, is shown to the left. (Based on photo by Lance Langford)

Fawning was a critical time in the reindeer industry: this was the chance for the herds to increase in size. The fawns were born in April and early May. The herders chose fawning grounds that would provide some protection from strong winds.

"We moved down to [Wolf] Creek for fawning. That's where the camp was. They had a spring they drank from. From March until about [the] first week in July they stayed there, and then they moved down to Kiglavak Bay."

David Roland (1992, Tape 53)

Every year some fawns would die. Some were stillborn, others were injured, and a few might be killed by predators or die when cold weather or blizzards set in. The fawning season presented challenges for the herders, and the reindeer had to be watched closely.

"In springtime, those yearlings went crazy. Where there was no snow, a bit of bare ground, they would go galloping—just playing around. The bulls would stay away from the females because they were fawning. So there were always two herds apart, and you had to watch them both. It would take more than one guy in spring [to keep them together]."

Peter Rufus (1991, Tape 20)

Fawning was also a time that some herders enjoyed. The days were getting longer and brighter, and life seemed a bit easier than during the long, dark days of winter.

"I'll tell you one thing. I kind of miss it. You know why? In springtime, when the reindeer were having fawns, I enjoyed it. In May it didn't get dark anymore. You went skiing where you wanted—and saw everything. I'd make an open fire, boil coffee—hot coffee. That was a very beautiful life, you know."

Jimmy Gordon (1992, Tape 4)

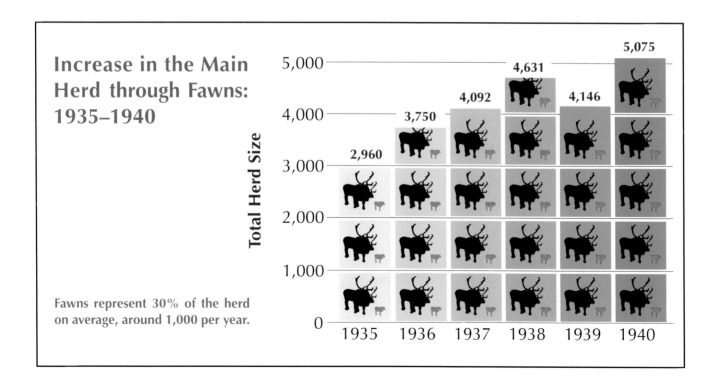

Increase in the Main Herd through Fawns: 1935–1940

Total Herd Size

Fawns represent 30% of the herd on average, around 1,000 per year.

| 1935 | 1936 | 1937 | 1938 | 1939 | 1940 |
| 2,960 | 3,750 | 4,092 | 4,631 | 4,146 | 5,075 |

Roundup!

Herd dashes into main holding area, trapped by herders at roundup near Kitigaaryuit, 1955. (Based on photo by D. Wilkinson/NWT Archives/N-1979-051-1146)

The roundup was one of the most exciting events of the year. This was the time to count, castrate, and earmark the reindeer herd, and to give them medicine if necessary. The roundup took place in July and August on the summer range. A corral and one or more pens were built for each Native herd.

People from around the area would come to help build the corral. Others just came to watch the excitement of driving, wrangling, and processing anywhere from 600 to several thousand reindeer. The government had a more permanent corral at Kidluit (Kiglavak) Bay.

"They helped from all over. From Reindeer Station and from the surrounding herds, they pitched in to help. The herders picked up all the logs along the beach and carried them by hand, walking back and forth and back and forth to get the corral built...Right before the roundup started was when they put up the corral. Right after they finished building it, they started herding the reindeer into the corral.

Every summer in July they had their roundup. To see if the herd had grown—to see if it was a smaller or larger herd—they counted all the reindeer that came through the corral.

They waited until they got all the reindeer into the corral, and they opened the small entrance to the fighting pen. Once they got them into the fighting pen, they castrated them, counted them, and marked their ears. They also counted the fawns and how many females and males there were."

Joseph Avik (1991, Tape 6)

Reindeer Roundup Corral

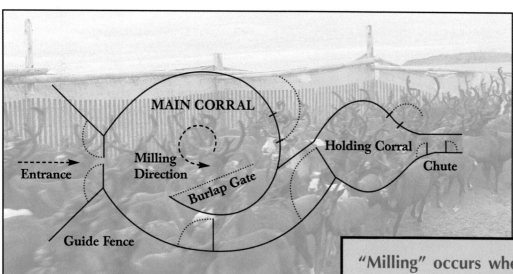

Reindeer circle in counterclockwise motion inside holding area of corral. Reindeer Depot, roundup, Mackenzie Delta. August 1955. (Based on photo by D. Wilkinson/NWT Archives/N-1979-051-1157)

"Milling" occurs when a herd runs in a circle in one direction. The reindeer do this to protect themselves. They run faster and faster, and the young reindeer wind up in the middle, with the faster-moving adults on the outside. Reindeer in Canada mill counterclockwise, and the corrals were designed to use this behaviour to direct the animals into the main corral. [23]

Roundup crew at Kidluit (Kiglavak) Bay, July 1937. Some Gwich'in men were hired to help with the roundup. Although the identity of many people is uncertain, Lazarus Sittichinli (second from left), Joseph (Yaya) Sittichinli (fourth from left, in front), and Joe Greenland (fifth from left), can be positively identified. (Based on photo by M. Meikle/National Archives of Canada/PA-203208)

The remains of the government corral at Kidluit (Kiglavak) Bay, 2000. (Elisa Hart, Courtesy of the Inuvialuit Land Administration)

"Just before corralling time, we drove the herd [to the corral]…After we [got] past the end of the fence, we held up the burlap and drove the herd in…and then closed it up again so they wouldn't get out. After they calmed down, we drove them again with the burlap into the small fighting pen. We kept on doing that for a few days until we were finished. The [reindeer] that were through already, we let run loose. Yes, everybody was helping each other."

Jimmy Komeak (1991, Tape 5)

"We used burlap as a fence to push them in. Once I fell down, and the whole herd came out…Nobody [was] there, and I just stood there. About 4,000–5,000 reindeer never even stepped on me. They just jumped—jumped without stepping on me. I thought I was a goner, but they never touched me!"

Otto Binder (1992, Tape 52)

Alice Smith (now French), Mary Pokiak, and Ruth Lucas at a roundup, August 1955. (Based on photo by D. Wilkinson/NWT Archives/N-1979-051-1130)

Herd Size from 1935 to 1967

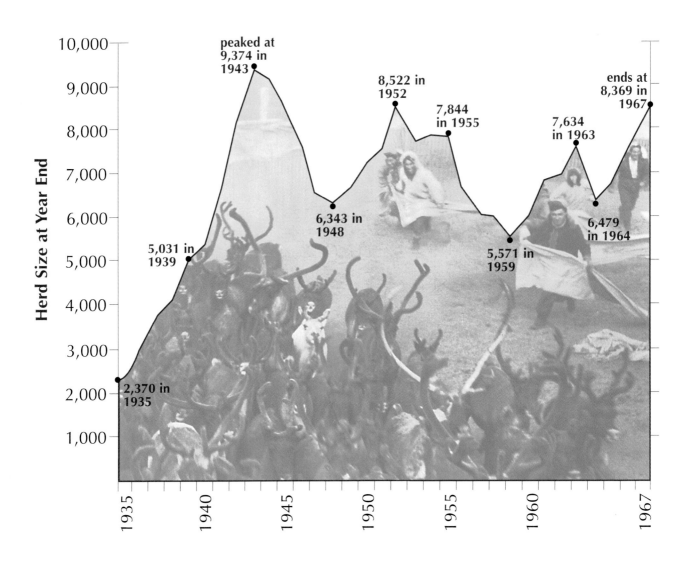

Herd Size at Year End

peaked at 9,374 in 1943

8,522 in 1952

7,844 in 1955

ends at 8,369 in 1967

7,634 in 1963

5,031 in 1939

6,343 in 1948

5,571 in 1959

6,479 in 1964

2,370 in 1935

Steers 25% 1,215

Cows 60% 2,990

Bulls 15% 870

Composition of the Main Herd in 1940 (5,076 reindeer)

Charlie Smith keeping records during a roundup, 1955. (Based on photo by D. Wilkinson/NWT Archives/N-1979-051-1562s)

Opposite page, bottom left: People watching the roundup action through the fence. (Based on photo by D. Wilkinson/ NWT Archives/N-1979-051-1152)

Peter Rufus, Jimmy Gordon, Adam Emaghok, and David Roland at roundup, 1955. (Based on photo by D. Wilkinson/NWT Archives/N-1979-051-1127)

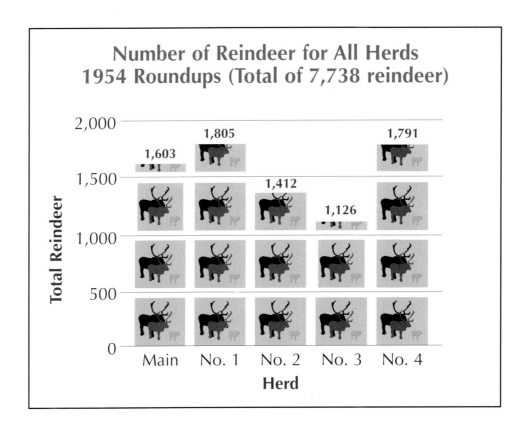

Adam Emaghok and Peter Rufus hold down a reindeer, while Wallace Lucas gives an injection. (Based on photo by D. Wilkinson/NWT Archives/N-1979-051-0348s)

Men and boys carry a reindeer through a pen at roundup, 1955. Unidentified boy, Donald Pingo, Adam Emaghok (behind reindeer), Peter Rufus, unidentified boy, and Ned Kayotuk. (Based on photo by D. Wilkinson/NWT Archives/N-1979-051-0354s)

"You got tired, especially when you tried to put [the reindeer] in the main corral...So we tried to put them in, [but] they didn't like to go in the corral. You had to keep running, or you'd lose them. [Then] you'd have to go back for them. It took days sometimes, to put them in the corral."

Adam Emaghok (2001, Tape 1)

"All the fawns that were...just born that spring, we...marked their ears. Every Native herd had a different earmark...There were four different Native herds at that time, No. 1, No. 2, No. 3, and No. 4...Every herd had its own mark."

Jimmy Komeak (1991, Tape 6)

Men mark a reindeer's ear. (Based on photo by D. Wilkinson/NWT Archives/N-1979-051-0351s)

The Annual Slaughter

Boys pushing a cart loaded with reindeer meat toward the Anglican school, Aklavik, 1940s. (Based on photo by M. Saich/NWT Archives/N-1990-003-116)

In the early days, the main herd was slaughtered on southern Richards Island in September. The meat was shipped to freezers in Aklavik.[24] A few reindeer were also slaughtered in winter for local use.

Later on, the main slaughter took place near Reindeer Station, and the time was changed to late fall or early winter, after freeze-up.

The meat was sold to the Anglican and Roman Catholic Missions in Aklavik for use in their schools and hospitals. Some of the meat was used for welfare, or "relief," as it was then called, and some was saved for the crew at Reindeer Station. Meat was also sold to Inuvialuit or others who could afford to buy it.[25]

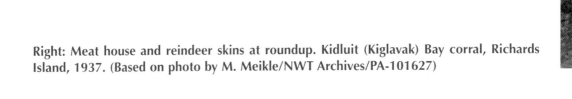

Right: Meat house and reindeer skins at roundup. Kidluit (Kiglavak) Bay corral, Richards Island, 1937. (Based on photo by M. Meikle/NWT Archives/PA-101627)

Number and Use of Slaughtered Reindeer in 1955

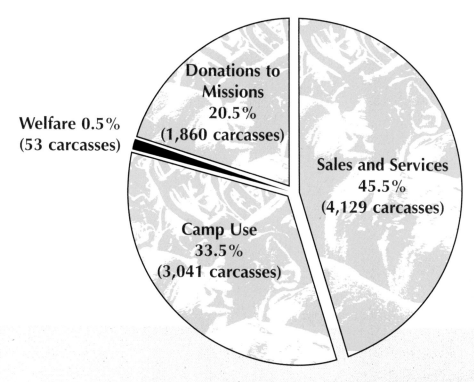

Donations to
Missions
20.5%
(1,860 carcasses)

Welfare 0.5%
(53 carcasses)

Sales and Services
45.5%
(4,129 carcasses)

Camp Use
33.5%
(3,041 carcasses)

Total of 9,083 carcasses (516,080 kilograms)

The herders and their families used fawn skins to make parkas or other clothing. Skins from sick fawns or those injured or killed during the roundup were used. The skins of the animals slaughtered in winter were sent to places in the Eastern Arctic where caribou were scarce at that time.[26]

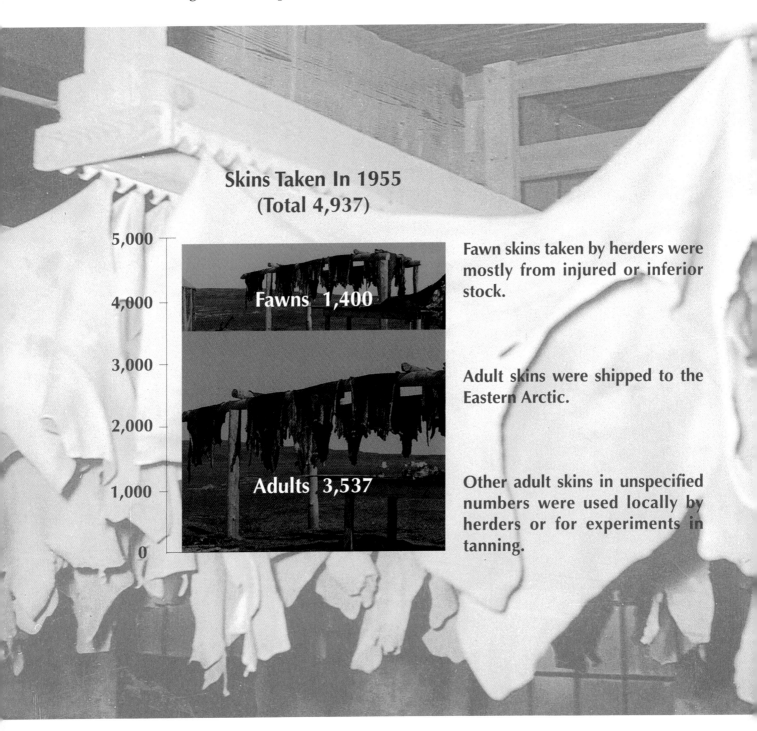

Skins Taken In 1955
(Total 4,937)

Fawns 1,400

Adults 3,537

Fawn skins taken by herders were mostly from injured or inferior stock.

Adult skins were shipped to the Eastern Arctic.

Other adult skins in unspecified numbers were used locally by herders or for experiments in tanning.

Among the Native herds, a slaughter was held once there were enough animals. The meat was transported to Aklavik. In later years, all animals to be slaughtered were sorted out of the Native herds at Eskimo (Husky) Lakes and then driven to Reindeer Station for slaughter.[27]

A large scow loaded with reindeer meat being pushed to the shore by a schooner, Aklavik, 1940s. (Based on photo by M. Saich/NWT Archives/N-1990-003-115)

In 1951, a meat-marketing plan was started. The Hudson's Bay Company was contracted to sell the meat.[28] The weight of a reindeer carcass was between 150 and 200 lbs (68–90.7 kg). In 1954, the price that Native managers were paid for reindeer meat was 35¢ per lb. (77¢ per kg).

The wholesale price was 41¢ per lb. (90¢ per kg), and retail prices in Aklavik, Tuktoyaktuk, and Reindeer Station were 52–62¢ per lb. ($1.15-$1.37 per kg).[29]

From 1935 to 1954, approximately 10,500 reindeer were used for meat and skins.[30]

Background image opposite page: Tanned reindeer skins. (Based on photo from Yellowknife Museum Society/NWT Archives/N-1979-055-0090)

A tractor with a load of reindeer meat at Reindeer Station, 1942. (Based on photo from the Yellowknife Museum Society/NWT Archives/N-1979-055-0088)

Keeping the Wolves Away!

Aslak Tornensis with a wolf killed near Reindeer Station in 1936. (Based on photo by A.L. Fleming/NWT Archives/N-1979-050-0303)

It was the herders' job to protect the reindeer from predators such as wolves, bears, and the occasional lynx. Wolves were seen as a big problem, but the number of wolf kills was not great.[31] It was suspected that wolves also caused losses of reindeer by making them stray while under attack. The herders were directed to stay on a constant lookout when wolves were around.

"Too many wolves at that time! [We] could kill them anytime [in] winter because they killed too much. [If] you left the reindeer for four hours, you'd lose about five...[The wolves would] stay around all the time with the reindeer. Well, at that time [there were] no caribou. When they had no caribou, [the wolves] stayed with reindeer all the time..."

Ned Kayotuk (1992, Tape 55)

Eva and William Apsimik, Inuvik, 1992. (Elisa Hart)

"They're bad anyway, those wolves...You could time them...Wolves have hours. From right at midnight until about 2:00 in the morning, they would go for their food...and then [from] between 4:00 and 5:00 until six o'clock in the morning. Those are their hours for killing reindeer...If you want to protect the reindeer, you've got to go out there at that time...You go out there and ski around them and make noises so the wolves don't get at the reindeer. If we had two guys, we took turns. When my turn came up, like it or not, I had to go."

William Apsimik (1992, Tape 54)

A barrenground grizzly bear. (Courtesy of Resources, Wildlife and Economic Development, Inuvik Region, GNWT)

"Especially the wolves used to kill the reindeer...One night...the wolves killed 14 reindeer, even though there were four herders, Edwin Allen, Jimmy [Komeak], Jimmy Nasuk (Nahogaloak), and me...After daylight came, we saw that our reindeer were scattered, but at least you could still see them. We had a cup of tea and headed for the reindeer. That was the largest kill—right across from Tunnunik on the mainland. It was in the fall time, right before freeze-up. All the wolves got away—it was hard for me to hunt wolves with no skis."

Joseph Avik (1992, Tape 9)

"Boy, at that time there used to be lots of wolves! With that herd at Anderson River and Reindeer Station, the wolves would go back and forth in a bunch. Maybe nine together, they went back and forth. When we had no wolves in the herd at Anderson River, there were lots at Reindeer Station. You knew they had moved there for a while. Boy, they killed lots. I remember one time they killed fourteen reindeer. They never ate them: they just killed them...When they are hungry, when there are four or five of them, they eat right away. But in a pack of about ten or eleven, they just kill for the fun of it."

Peter Rufus (1991, Tape 20)

Bears were not seen to be as big a problem as wolves. They seemed to be a problem only during the fawning season.

"The bears are pretty bad in spring at fawning time. Boy, they could kill lots, too. They cached them for later on."

Peter Rufus (1991, Tape 20)

Lynx were not much of a problem, but every now and then some would get a taste for reindeer.

"There were a couple of lynx that killed reindeer around Inuksivik. There were three at the time. That's when they killed two reindeer. After they killed the reindeer, they buried them in the snow. They were adult reindeer and they buried them. It was mid-winter. We killed them right away as they kept coming around, those three lynx."

Joseph Avik (1992, Tape 9)

Lynx rarely preyed on reindeer, but when they did, it made a memorable story. (Courtesy of Resources, Wildlife and Economic Development, Inuvik Region, GNWT)

The Thrills and Spills of Learning to Ski

Jimmy Gordon, holding his skis, stands beside a pile of antlers near Reindeer Station. (Courtesy of Jimmy Gordon)

Skis were an important part of a herder's equipment. In winter, the herders wore skis to move around on the land and to herd the reindeer. The skis were made of wood, and the herders put skins on them to make it easier to walk up hills. They used only one pole. Elders recalled with laughter the thrills, spills, and pain of learning to ski.

> **"The first day I was hired, I had to ski out to the herd: fifteen miles. I'd never skied in my life before. Boy! When I got to the herd, I stayed in the tent for two days because my legs were so tired!"**
>
> **David Roland (1992, Tape 53)**

Background image opposite page: Reindeer arrive at Kuururyuaq, March 1935. (Based on photo by R. Terpening/NWT Archives/N-1987-030-0465)

"I put on my skis and started to try to learn to ski downhill. When I started going too fast, I fell down. I was scared I was going to crash...I thought to myself, I'm going to make it this time! I made up my mind I was going to make it. I was just about at the bottom of the hill. I'd just about made it when I fell down...so I took my skis off and started walking up the hill...When I did make it, I thought it was fun! I had to learn, and that's how I learned."

Danny Sydney (1992, Tape 3)

Danny Sydney of Inuvik in the 1980s.
(Courtesy of Danny Sydney)

"Edwin Allen taught me to ski, and it didn't take long to learn. I learned from just watching. But when you first got on [the skis], you couldn't stay on and were forever falling down. After you learned, it was no bother. I was so mischievous I learned pretty fast."

Joseph Avik (1992, Tape 9)

Some of the herders recall their daredevil experiences in skiing from the top of a hill behind Reindeer Station. They would go so fast that they were barely in control. For those who hadn't done it before, it was a hair-raising experience.

"I [went] right from the top [of the hill] to see how fast I would go, but the trails were so crooked! I started down and I was going so fast! I thought I'd fall down, but I thought I would hurt myself just trying to stay on my feet. Well, I kept steadying myself, and before I knew it, I was across the river. After a little while, my legs were just aching! I'll never try that again!"

Joseph Avik (1992, Tape 9)

"Yes, [they raced] down that hill, but I never was good at it. I kept away from it as much as I could. I didn't want to break my neck! But some guys...right from the top, they made it across. Some places are pretty steep. Wallace Lucas was good at that."

David Roland (1992, Tape 53)

Working with Reindeer

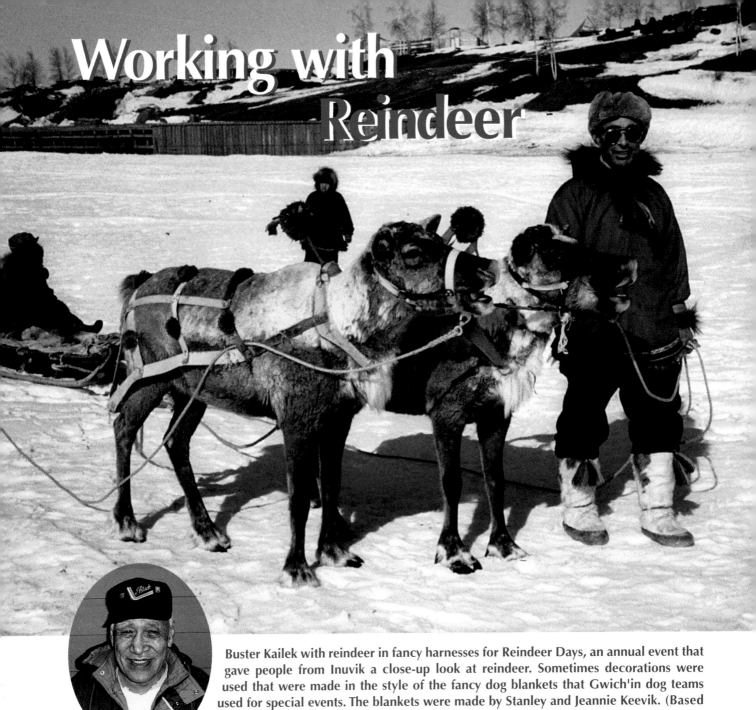

Buster Kailek with reindeer in fancy harnesses for Reindeer Days, an annual event that gave people from Inuvik a close-up look at reindeer. Sometimes decorations were used that were made in the style of the fancy dog blankets that Gwich'in dog teams used for special events. The blankets were made by Stanley and Jeannie Keevik. (Based on photo by © R.C. Knights/NWT Archives/N-1993-002-009)

Stanley Keevik (Harmony Marcotte)

"When we first picked a reindeer to train, we looked through the herd to see which one would be good for pulling. Then we lassoed it and tied it to a pole with a really short rope. We let it stay tied up, sometimes overnight, sometimes not even that long. Then we untied it and started pulling the reindeer toward us. When it started taking a few steps toward you, you led it around. Once it started following, you put a harness on it. When we first put on the harness, [the reindeer] was nervous. It wouldn't stay still and it jumped all over. Then when they got used to it, we tied the reindeer to the sled. We trained it and trained it. Some learned in one day, some [took] three, four days or longer. Some of them learned really fast, just like dogs."

Joseph Avik (1992, Tape 9)

Handling and training reindeer was an important part of a herder's job. Reindeer were used to pull sleds in winter, and they could carry loads in packs in summer. In the early days, sled dogs were seldom used, as managers feared that they might attack the reindeer.

In learning to become herders, trainees had to train the reindeer to wear a harness and pull a sled. Some reindeer were cooperative, but trying to train such large animals could often be difficult. Some herders found it easier than others.

Danny Smith struggles with a reindeer at Ren Lake near Inuvik. Spring, 1965. (Dick Hill)

Some reindeer were considered difficult for various reasons. Some were lazy and slow moving, and some were stubborn and would not move at all. Others were dangerous.

"Once they lie down, they won't get up. They won't get up and you have to curse away. No matter how much you slap or coax them, they won't get up. There is nothing you can do, so you tie it and eventually it gets up by itself."

Joseph Avik (1992, Tape 9)

Sleds are loaded and ready to go. Reindeer Station in the1930s. (Based on photo by R. Terpening/NWT Archives/ N-1987-030-0471)

Reindeer hitched to sled. No date. (Based on photo by A.L. Fleming/NWT Archives/N-1979-050-0309)

"They're just like a lazy dog. When they're lazy, they're slow walking. When some of them lie down, you can hardly make them move."

Nellie Lester (1992, Tape 5/6)

"Those that are not dangerous have their antlers left on. Those that are dangerous, they cut the antlers off."

Joseph Avik (1992, Tape 7)

"Some are easy to use, but some are kind of rough, too. Same as anything else, like dogs or humans. Some are wild and they stay that way, and you can't make them any better. Some, you can jump on their back. When the reindeer have learned, they will follow you. Even if they have no ropes, they follow behind you. "

Jimmy Komeak (1991, Tape 9)

Some herders found that reindeer were easier to keep than dogs. Reindeer could be turned loose to feed, but you had to bring food for dogs.

"You just let your reindeer go. If you needed them, you could catch them again. Not the young ones, not the fawns, and not the females: just the castrated males were the only kind that we used for pulling, or to move around."

Jimmy Komeak (1991, Tape 9)

Reindeer could make a herder's life easier in summer, too.

"If we had to move for one or two weeks [in summer], we used reindeer packing. Just like a dog [but with] big packs. After they learned, oh boy, they were really good!"

Jimmy Komeak (1991, Tape 9)

Reindeer had a recreational side, as well: some of the herders liked to race them.

"At New Year's and Christmas, we had fun with them. We used them for racing."

Joseph Avik (1992, Tape 7)

Silas Kangegana and his team of reindeer in the 1940s. (Courtesy of Ruth and Ishmael Alunik)

Reindeer and Caribou

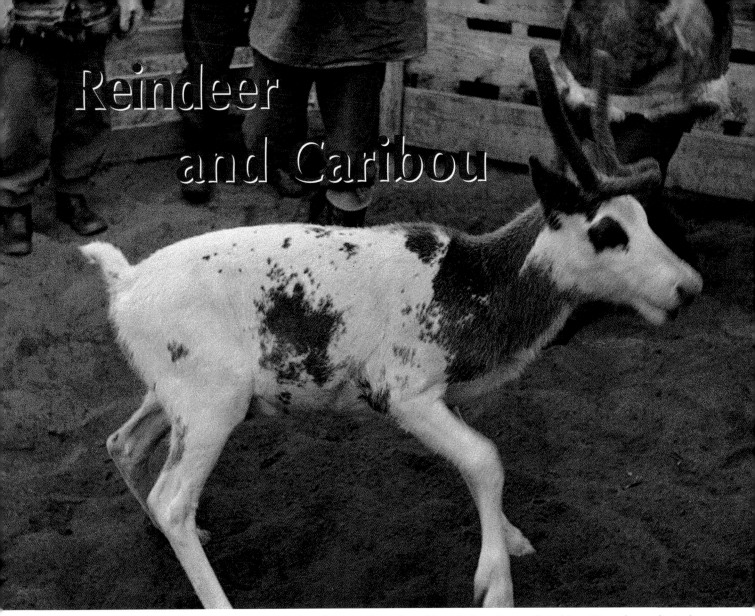

Reindeer show more colour variation than caribou do. This reindeer is nearly white. (Based on photo by D. Wilkinson/NWT Archives/N-1979-051-1153)

There is some debate amongst herders about whether you can tell the difference between caribou and reindeer. Caribou are wild animals in the New World, in northern North America and Greenland. Reindeer occur in the northern parts of the Old World, such as Siberia, Sweden and Norway. Because caribou and reindeer have been separated for thousands of years, they have become a bit different in the way they behave and, in some cases, in the way they look.

The reindeer that were brought from Alaska to Canada were originally from Siberia. They had been domesticated, and because of that they acted differently from the caribou. Most important for the herding industry, reindeer are easier to control and to tame than caribou.

Many former reindeer herders say that it was easy to tell the difference between caribou and reindeer, and that it was easy to spot a caribou in the reindeer herd. They noticed both behavioural and physical differences. The reindeer are less alert than caribou, which are always on the watch for predators, and therefore have their heads up more than reindeer.

"There is a lot of difference. The reindeer have shorter legs and are a different colour—darker, and spotted shades. If I saw a caribou among my herd, I could see it from a long way. They stick way up over everything. The caribou has a different back belly—in reindeer it's darker. The caribou has shorter antlers that are closer together, but the reindeer's are far apart."

Jimmy Komeak (1991, Tape 9)

It was the herders' job to keep the caribou away from the reindeer.

"If a caribou got mixed up with our reindeer, we killed it. Otherwise, that caribou could make the herd stray."

Jimmy Komeak (1991, Tape 9)

The mating season of caribou is about six to eight weeks later than that of reindeer.[32] For this reason, the herd supervisors didn't think there would be much of a problem with caribou and reindeer interbreeding. However, if a reindeer cow didn't breed during her mating season, she might come into heat again later and be receptive to a caribou bull.

When the reindeer were brought to the Mackenzie Delta, there were very few caribou around. Now there are many. Some elders think that the reindeer brought the caribou back to the area. Others think that the animals we see now are a cross between caribou and reindeer.

English Name	Scientific Name	Siglitun Name[33]
Reindeer	*Rangifer tarandus tarandus*	qun'ngiq
Barrenground Caribou	*Rangifer tarandus groenlandicus*	tuktu

Those Wonderful Herding Dogs

"A person without dogs suffers. When they were big enough, you'd take them herding every day, so the dog would get used to you. You trained them slowly. Later on, when they got older, they got better: you made your sign [hand signal], and they went to get the herd. Your dog gets better every year. They watch you to see where you want them to go."

Jimmy Komeak (1992, Tape 9)

Chahpy, a border collie, is the type of dog used for reindeer herding. Chahpy belongs to the Binder family of Inuvik. (Elisa Hart)

Border collies were brought from Alaska to use in herding the reindeer. Herders had to learn to work with the dogs and train them to respond to a whistle and to hand signals. It was clear that a good herd dog made a herder's job a lot easier. The dogs were used to keep the herd together and bring it to the herder. This meant that the herder did not have to walk or ski so much.

"Once they are trained, you can [direct] them with your arms to tell them which way you want them to go. You just whistle at them and they keep going. Edwin Allen taught me how to train herd dogs. He said, 'While you're training them, you're going to have a hard time. You are going to do a lot of walking.' The dog could smell [the reindeer] by their tracks. With [dogs] that are well trained, when you send them, you can stay in one place. So I did that. I just stayed in one place, and the whole herd [was brought] to me."

Jimmy Komeak (1991, Tape 9)

"I trained the dog myself—just a little pup. I carried him all the time...While I was teaching the dog, Felix Pagnana would command his dog to go to the herd or direct him to come, and that's how I started training my dog...I unleashed him when he was half trained, and finally he started going by himself. Little by little, he started going further and further. It doesn't take long if you train them when they're little.

After it was full-grown, it was well trained. I would take it out alone, and when I yelled at it, it came right back. It was so obedient it would turn back, waiting for a command, and I would motion it to go or come back. The dog was so well trained it would go to the highest hill to see which way I would direct it. He couldn't hear my voice up there. Sometimes he was so far, he couldn't see my arms, so I took my parki off and I would signal 'come' or 'go' and he would do it. That was my only dog that was really well trained, because he would bring the reindeer back to me.

The following year, the dog got a bone stuck in his throat and died. I didn't know what to do, so I quit herding reindeer for a while after I lost my dog. I was hurt for quite a while and didn't go herding. After a few weeks they asked me to come back, so I did. I had another dog, but it wasn't quite the same as the one I trained. When you train your own, they are the best dogs."

Joseph Avik (1992, Tape 9)

Mikkel Pulk's dog Kobuk watches the herd on the fawning grounds on Richards Island, 1936. (Based on photo by J.A. Urquehart/National Archives of Canada/PA-121721)

Graham Douglas, Hiram Oscar, Ned Kayotuk, and Mikkel Pulk. (Based on photo by E. Watt/NWT Archives/ N-1990-005-487)

An Enjoyable Life

Most people who tried reindeer herding did not stay with it for long. However, some herders worked at it for years. Despite the hardships, they enjoyed the lifestyle and the little things that made their lives satisfying.

"In the herding days, when we had nothing to do in the evening, and it got dark and was getting quiet, we stayed in the tent. The older guys used to tell stories. Boy, I liked that."

Jimmy Komeak (1991, Tape 9)

"I remember the time when we were up in Husky Lakes just after Christmas, in January. We were living in a tent at that time, and the tent had little holes…[When] you turned the light off, you could see the stars.

You had to keep the stove going day and night to keep yourself warm, at least if you didn't want everything to freeze at night…When you woke up in the morning, sometimes the pots were cracking. Yes, and then when you lit the stove, you felt like living again. It was a hard life, but it was an enjoyable life…It was fun."

William Apsimik (1992, Tape 54)

Camp life at Kidluit (Kiglavak) Bay. On the right, Mikkel Pulk and his dog Kobuk sit by the tent. Wallace Lucas (in white parka) stands next to a tent. The other people are unidentified. (Based on photo by I.S. Hadwen/NWT Archives/N-1979-567)

The pay was low, but with the rations it was enough to make some herders feel secure.

"We got $25.00 a month, but we never bought meat: we had rations all the time. Just clothing we bought...we had two kids at that time, when we stayed down there. Twenty-five dollars a month...We miss some of [those things]...I wish we could go back sometimes. Back to those skis (laugh). It's safe when you travel with skis all the time. There are no breakdowns."
Ned Kayotuk (1992, Tape 55)

Donald and Ida Silaotsiak with children Julia and Peter, 1949–1950. Donald was said to be one of the fastest cross-country skiers. (Courtesy of Peter Silaotsiak)

Susanna and Aslak Tornensis at their tent. (Based on photo by R. Terpening/NWT Archives/N-1987-030-0470)

Some herders were very dedicated and took pride in the work they did.

"When you learn it and do it for so long, you know your duty. You knew when your turn came up, you had to get out there and look after them. You look after them the best you can—you put your heart into it. [You] put everything into it."

William Apsimik (1992, Tape 54)

Janson Oksoasiak was a herder in the Anderson River area. His son Donald (opposite page) was also a herder. (Courtesy of Nellie Pokiak)

The First "Native" Herds

Charlie Rufus holding a fawn three-and-a-half months old, Native Herd No. 1, Nicholson Island, August 1943. (Based on photo by J.A. Parsons/National Archives of Canada/PA-500043)

As the main herd grew and a number of herders were trained, the government wanted to start creating "Native" herds. Each Native herd was to be managed by two men. One would own a schooner, which could be used to transport people and supplies to the grazing areas.[34] A government supervisor would stay with them until it was clear that the herd and herders were doing well.

> "Peter [Kaglik] liked it because we couldn't afford anything. We were so poor we had no white man's food. Even though it didn't pay well, he took the job. They gave us rations."
>
> Mary Avik (1992, Tape 9)

Charlie Kitli (Rufus) and Rufus Kalialuk

Of the local men who trained as herders, Charlie Rufus was the first chosen to manage a herd. His partner was his father, Rufus Kalialuk, who owned a schooner. The government decided that a father and son would work well together as herd owners. In 1938, the government lent them 950 reindeer to take to their grazing grounds near the Anderson

Rufus Kalialuk (Based on photo from © ISDP/Martha Harry Collection/15)

River. Stanley Mason went along as the departmental supervisor.[35] They did very well, and by 1942 they had 2,473 reindeer, of which 950 were to be returned to the government.[36]

A cabin at the mouth of the Anderson River. Built for the superintendent of the Anderson River operation, it was later used by the Canadian Wildlife Service. (Elisa Hart)

Peter Kaglik and Amos Tumma

In 1940, the second Native herd was started. Peter Kaglik and Amos Tumma were the new managers. Peter was already a herder, and Amos owned a schooner. Their herd, which occupied grounds east of the Anderson River, was sometimes referred to as the Horton River herd. They received 825 reindeer on loan.[37]

The two Native herds were doing well until disaster struck in 1944. Eleven people were killed when the Rufus boat, the *Calla*, sank in one of the worst storms in years. All the herd managers, some children, and the field supervisor were drowned. After the accident, the two herds were joined, but many reindeer could not be found.

Amos Tumma in the early 1970s. (Courtesy of Colin Amos)

"**Four thousand animals strayed when the people drowned. We only found 40, but in winter we found 2,000 at Husky Bend, and they were mixed in with caribou. After that, there were lots of caribou."**

Edgar Kotokak (1991, Tape 25)

The accident was a serious blow for the reindeer industry. It became increasingly difficult for the government to find men who wanted to manage a herd. Men with schooners were already successful trappers and did not need the work. Being a herd owner was a lot of responsibility, and managers could not always leave the herd to go hunting. They had reindeer to eat, but there was little financial reward. Some herders were uncomfortable with the idea of having to be the boss of other men. It was clear that the government would need to make changes to attract men to the industry.[38]

Mary and Peter Kaglik with their adopted son Oscar (formerly an Illasiak). (Based on photo by J. A. Parsons/ National Archives of Canada/PA-101092)

The remains of the Rufus/Kalialuk corral on Nicholson Island, 1995. (Elisa Hart)

Ellen Binder, Donald Pingo (behind), Joseph Avik, Mary Avik, and Jimmy Komeak at Reindeer Station, July 1992. (Elisa Hart)

Improving Conditions for Herd Managers

To make the job of herd manager more attractive, the government changed some of its practices. Managers would now get rations for a longer time, and the government would help with transportation by lending managers a freighter canoe. The government would also pay the wages of herding assistants for the managers for two to three years.[39] Herders would have to return only half of the reindeer lent to them after three years, and the government would take care of marketing and transporting the reindeer meat. The reindeer reserve was extended to cover approximately 46,361 km²–almost three times its original area.[40] Perhaps the most important change was grazing the herds closer to Reindeer Station and the communities, so that the manager, the herders, and their families would not be so isolated.

Otto Binder and Jimmy Nahogaloak

A third Native herd, managed by Otto Binder and Jimmy Nahogaloak (also known as Nasuk), was started with 878 reindeer in late 1948. It was called Native Herd No. 1. Otto and Jimmy kept their herd in the Eskimo (Husky) Lakes area and had a corral not far from the old village of Kitigaaryuit and another in Husky Lakes. In 1952 their partnership ended, and the herd was returned to the government.[41]

Jimmy Nahogaloak in the early 1980s. Jimmy was co-manager of a reindeer herd with Otto Binder, but later returned to Cambridge Bay. (Courtesy of Charles Nahogaloak)

Wallace Lucas and Peter Rufus

A fourth herd, Native Herd No. 2, was started when Wallace Lucas and Peter Rufus were lent 1,099 reindeer in February 1950. They kept the herd west of Tuktoyaktuk near Qiniqsiq in summer and further south in Eskimo (Husky) Lakes for the rest of the year. Their herd did very well and grew to such a number that they returned enough reindeer to the government to meet the terms of their contract. This made them the first official Inuvialuit or Inuit owners of reindeer in Canada. Their partnership ended in 1956.[42]

Wallace Lucas, herd owner, 1955. (Based on photo by D. Wilkinson/NWT Archives/N-1979-051-1144)

Jimmy Komeak and Guy Omilgoituk

The fifth herd, started with a loan of 825 reindeer in 1952, was managed by Jimmy Komeak and Guy Omilgoituk. It was called Herd No. 3, and their corral was near Toker Point.[43]

Roundup at Wallace Lucas and Peter Rufus' corral near Tuktoyaktuk, ca.1951. (Based on photo by T. Hunt/ NWT Archives/N-1979-062-0023)

> "At Toker Point we spent the summer for about three months. Twelve months a year we moved. I didn't like to get too close to another herd. I didn't like that there was No. 4 herd over there [near Warren Point]...I tried to keep them apart...We didn't go too far because we had no machines. In summertime they didn't eat moss anyway. They ate fresh grass. When summer was over, we moved back to Husky Lakes. Our winter camp was at Old Man Lake."
>
> **Jimmy Komeak (1991, Tape 24)**

This herd did well at first, but the numbers started dropping and eventually it was returned to the government. There was good money to be made in the area with the construction of sites for the DEW Line (Distant Early Warning Line), and the oil companies were starting exploration. The herd was returned in 1956.

"I owned a herd for five years. The first three summers, there were more fawns. The two last summers the herd didn't grow: there weren't enough females. When we cut the herd off from the government herd, there were not enough females—mostly bulls, yearlings, whatever. That's why [the herd] didn't grow. So I gave up there...After I gave it up, after 1956, the DEW Line started, Imperial Oil, and other companies. They started to [pay] good money."

Jimmy Komeak (1991, Tape 24)

Guy Omilgoituk in the mid 1970s. (Courtesy of Ann Kasook)

The remains of the corral that belonged to Jimmy Komeak and Guy Omilgoituk, near Toker Point, 1995. (John Poirier)

Herd owners Donald Pingo and Adam Emaghok hold down a reindeer at a roundup in 1955. (Based on photo by D. Wilkinson/NWT Archives/N-1979-051-1563s)

Donald Pingo and Adam Emaghok

A sixth Native herd was started in 1953 by Donald Pingo and Adam Emaghok. They took over animals from the Binder-Nahogaloak herd in addition to 950 reindeer. Their grazing area was near Kitigaaryuit in summer and near Eskimo (Husky) Lakes in winter. The herd was returned in 1955.[44]

Wallace Lucas and Adam Emaghok

After the Binder and Nahogaloak herd and the Pingo and Emaghok herds were returned to the government, they were combined in 1956 and managed by Wallace Lucas and Adam Emaghok for a year.[45]

Joseph Avik and Bob Panaktalok

The seventh herd, called herd No. 4 at the time, was managed by Joseph Avik and Bob Panaktalok starting in 1954. They received 1,302 reindeer, which they summered near Warren Point and wintered on the south side of Eskimo (Husky) Lakes. They kept their herd for 10 years before returning it in 1964. This was the longest that anyone had owned a herd up to that time.[46]

The corral that was used by Otto Binder and Jimmy Nahogaloak and later by Adam Emaghok and Donald Pingo. It is located near the old village of Kitigaaryuit. (D. Wilkinson/NWT Archives/N-1979-051-0360s)

Bombardier taking supplies to reindeer camps, 1959. (Based on photo by E. Watt/NWT Archives/N-1990-005-0483)

The remains of the corral that belonged to Joseph Avik and Bob Panaktalok, near Warren Point, 1995. (John Poirier)

The remains of the fighting pen at the corral owned by Joseph Avik and Bob Panaktalok, near Warren Point, 1991. (Elisa Hart)

Reindeer Station

Loading sleds to move out to reindeer camps. Reindeer Station, early 1940s. (Based on photo by A.L. Fleming/NWT Archives/N-1979-050-313)

Reindeer Station was the base of operations for the reindeer industry. The superintendent and maintenance staff lived there, and there were also houses for herders and their families and sheds for equipment and supplies. Over time, the Station turned into a community, with a school, a store, and a church.

When most elders speak of Reindeer Station, they recall a place where the living was good. With their own houses, rations, and pay, the herders and their families were more financially secure than trappers when the fur prices were low or the hunting was bad.[47]

In the early days, the wives and children of the herders would stay at Reindeer Station while the men herded in fall and winter.

"There were a lot of people at Reindeer Station...they brought us women there after we left our husbands, when they looked after the reindeer herd in the fall."

Rhoda Allen (1992, Tape 1)

Opposite page: A view of the remains of Reindeer Station and the Delta beyond. Tom Smith and Hiram Oscar in the foreground, 1992. (Naudia Lennie)

Although the women were left on their own to look after the children while the men were off herding, there were few reports of loneliness.

"I stayed with his family when he went out herding. They were like my real parents. My in-laws were good to me, so I didn't mind staying with them at Reindeer Station. I didn't speak a word of English. Eventually I understood a bit."

Mary Avik (1992, Tape 10)

Since it was hard to attract men to herding because of the isolation, it was decided that the men should live at Reindeer Station in winter and herd in shifts.

"We spent the winter at Reindeer Station. We would take turns to go herd the reindeer. Sometimes there would be three of us, sometimes four of us, one week at a time."

Danny Sydney (1992, Tape 3)

Reindeer Station in the summer of 1937. The white house was used by the manager. The smaller cabins in the back were for herders. (Photographer unknown/© National Archives of Canada/PA-203204)

"Everybody went to Reindeer Station—all the families. Just the men went out in shifts. Once we got to the Station, sometimes we stayed out three to four nights. Then another shift came and took our place."

David Roland (1992, Tape 53)

Reindeer Station was not only a secure place to live. The elders also recall what a great social life they had there.

"Reindeer Station was an excellent station at one time! Oh, yes, lots of fun! We were young at that time (laugh). Lots of activities, games and stuff."

William Apsimik (1992, Tape 54)

"Lots of dances in those days, you know. Everybody danced, and there was no whisky. We danced right until morning sometimes—square dancing and fiddling."

Jimmy Komeak (1991, Tape 9)

"Oh, boy! We used to have lots of activities there long ago. After work in the evenings, we'd visit around and play games."

David Roland (1992, Tape 53)

Education was important at Reindeer Station. A school was built and a teacher was hired. Classes were held at night for adults so they could study reading, writing, and arithmetic.[48] However, schooling at Reindeer Station was dependent on government funding:

"When the government sold the reindeer to someone else—when the Wildlife [Canadian Wildlife Service] started to look after them—they didn't have enough money to keep the school open. They had money to look after the reindeer, but had no money for the school."

Danny Sydney (1992, Tape 6)

A later version of the type of cabin that herders and their families lived in at Reindeer Station. Some former herders laughed at seeing this photograph. They had thought the cabins were big when they first moved in, because they were used to living in tents. (Elisa Hart)

Buildings at Reindeer Station—1955

5 residences for white employees
1 cabin for Chief Herder
7 cabins for herders
1 large warehouse
3 small warehouses

1 workshop
1 garage for D4 tractor and bombardier
1 building to house the electric lighting plant
and firefighting equipment

Transportation Equipment

3 schooners or motor boats
1 admiral speed boat
1 bombardier

1 barge
2 scows
several canoes

Below: Door to the ice house at Reindeer Station, 1992. (Elisa Hart)

Roy Saglu and Nels Pulk in the 1950s with ice from the ice house at Reindeer Station. (Courtesy of Ruth and Ishmael Alunik)

A bird's-eye view of Reindeer Station. Probably taken in the 1960s. (Based on photo by S. Johansson/NWT Archives/N-1987-028-CN29)

It is clear from the comments of the elders that Reindeer Station was a special place.

"To make a living, you've got to work for it. That's what Reindeer Station was made for...the women stayed there and we worked for ourselves—for the family."

William Apsimik (1992, Tape 54)

"We had happy times here because everyone was treated the same. We were all issued a tent and a stove and rations every month and reindeer to eat. Everyone was happy. No one was higher up than anyone else."

Ellen Binder (1992, Tape 11)

A Family Experience

A group of people at roundup. Malcolm McNabb, Lennie Lucas, Wallace Lucas, Johnny Aviugana (behind), Mikkel Pulk, Anna Pulk (behind), Ellen Pulk (in front), Emma Aviugana holding child (behind), Christina Aviugana, Ruby Stringer, Ruth Lucas, unidentified woman standing behind, two unidentified boys, unidentified woman holding child, Alex Illasiak in front, Aggie Illasiak holding Oscar, 1941. (Based on photo by M. Meikle/National Archives of Canada/PA-203209)

Reindeer herding was a way of life for the entire family. Husbands were often gone for long periods of time while they were herding. Wives were sometimes left alone at camps, or had the friendship of others at Reindeer Station. Sometimes the entire family travelled with the herd and moved camp as needed. Some women and children learned to ski, herd, and drive reindeer. It was a real family experience.

The names of the families that elders remembered are listed throughout this section. These are the names of the herders and their families who were involved in the early days of the reindeer industry, from 1935 to the early 1960s. Our apologies to anyone whose name was forgotten.

Oscar

Tedjuk

Kunuk

Omilgoituk

Saglu

Ayak

Nahogaloak

Pingo

Natin

Noksana

Avingayoak (Avik)

Tumma

Smith

Allen

Komeak

Kangegana

Toklak

Maksagak

Kikoak

Silaotsiak

Tardiff

Amagonalok

Aviugana

Gus Tardiff and his daughters, Emily (on his arm) and Mona, in the late 1940s. (Courtesy of Andy Tardiff)

Nels Pulk and the Rufus children. Peter, Colin (front), Albert, and Millie, 1940. The latter three children drowned in 1944, when their boat, the *Calla*, sank in a storm while heading back to the herd at Anderson River. (Based on a photo by W.E. Hogan/National Archives of Canada/PA-500045)

Kailek   Binder

          Emaghok

Keevik   Gordon

          Ovayuak

Sittichinli

               Panaktalok

Madeline Smith, Inuvik, 1992. (Naudia Lennie)

                    Sydney

     Pagnana

                    Kaliałuk

Aneroluk   Apsimik

Reindeer herders give dog team rides at Long Lake, near Inuvik, in 1964. (Dick Hill)

Kayotuk

Rufus

Raymond

Pulk

Illasiak

Ruth Lucas and Jeannie Keevik outside the corral near Tuktoyaktuk that belonged to Wallace Lucas and Peter Rufus. (Based on photo by T. Hunt/NWT Archives/N-1979-062-0019)

Kotokak

Tornensis

Haetta

Roland

Lucas

Kaglik

Mangelana

Oscar

Pokiak

Havgun

Oksoasiak

Local Concerns About the Reindeer Industry

DEPARTMENT OF
MINES AND RESOURCES

Lands, Parks and
Forests Branch

ADMINISTRATION
of the
NORTHWEST TERRITORIES
CANADA

Permit No. 208

PERMIT

TO ENTER REINDEER GRAZING RESERVE

(Issued under the Reindeer Protection Ordinance and Regulations)

Subject to the laws and regulations applicable to the Northwest Territories now

or hereafter in force, authority is hereby granted to..

....of...

to enter the Kittigazuit Reindeer Grazing Reserve for the purpose of

This permit expires on the........................day of...19.5.,
and must be returned to the Superintendent as soon as practicable thereafter.

Please note that this permit does not allow any hunting and trapping privileges on or
around Richards Island.

I accept this permit on the above terms.

....
Permittee

Issued at...

....
Issuing Officer

Date... (Title)...

NOTE—Any person who violates any of the provisions of the regulations under which this permit is issued may be
prosecuted under that part of the Criminal Code relating to summary convictions, being Part XV of the Revised Statutes of
Canada, 1927, Chapter 36, before a Justice of the Peace, or before any officer of the Royal Canadian Mounted Police empowered
by law to sit and act as a Justice of the Peace.
R-3299

A copy of the permit that was required to enter the Reindeer Grazing Reserve. (The Glenbow–Alberta Institute/NWT Archives/N-1995-004 File 2-3)

Not all Inuvialuit were pleased with the way the reindeer industry had turned out. Some had believed that when the reindeer arrived, they could be killed for meat. They did not realize they would have to buy them. After all, the reindeer were like caribou, which people could hunt whenever they wanted. The price of reindeer meat was also higher than many could afford.[49]

> "One reindeer [carcass] was $25.00. Some of them were $21.00. But that was a lot of money for us at that time because we didn't have much money. Fur was cheap; [it paid] just enough to get along."
>
> **Peter Rufus (1991, Tape 20)**

The presence of the reindeer also meant that people needed a permit to go onto land that they had always used for hunting and trapping. This caused a lot of resentment and frustration.

> "You could [trap on the reserve], but you had to have a permit. It was the bureaucracy that bothered them; there was no cost for the permit."
>
> **Ellen Binder (1992, Tape 10)**

Reindeer were located in areas where people from Tuktoyaktuk trapped marten, mink, and muskrat. Trappers were frustrated because they felt that the reindeer were destroying their muskrat trapping areas. The reindeer were thought to break the muskrat houses to eat the grass they are made of.[50]

> "People used to depend on hunting and trapping...In those days trappers didn't like their area spoiled, and reindeer used to scratch the ground."
>
> **Jimmy Komeak (1992, Tape 10)**

For these reasons, there was sometimes tension between some Inuvialuit and the government over the reindeer.

The End of the Native Herds

Dew Line Station, Tuktoyaktuk, 1995. (John Poirier)

No further Native herds were created after 1956. The Avik and Panaktalok herd was allowed to keep going until the partnership ended in 1964. For a number of reasons the herds were not growing, but shrinking. The total number of reindeer loaned for Native herds was 7,032, and the total number returned was 3,315.[51]

There was too much competition from well-paid jobs on the DEW Line and elsewhere to attract men to herding. The herding life did not provide much of an income. The lack of success of the Native herds showed that herding was not a stable or predictable way to make a living. It was too isolating and presented too many hardships. Given the competition from salaried jobs, most people did not want to settle for the lower standard of living of a herder.

Reindeer herding was not a way to earn a large income. The wages for herding had increased over the years from about $20 to $90 per month. Even with rations, this wage was low. The government's plan had been to create self-sufficient herding units that would not need government support. But the income of a herder or a herd owner could not compete with the wages being paid by the new employers in the area. The building of the DEW Line, the building of Inuvik, and the early oil exploration initiatives all paid very well. There was little reason to stay with reindeer herding when you could earn a herder's yearly income in a week.

"I remember when I got my first roll from the DEW Line: $180. Oh, big money! Two weeks' wages!...Yes, I worked seven days a week as a cat operator—lots of overtime! [It] was two dollars and ten cents an hour regular time and double time on Sunday. Saturday was time and a half. I came home with $2,100 in cheques, and I had another $1,000 coming to me. Besides that, I sent my wife I don't know how many cheques at that time. I bought a 10-horse outboard motor [and a] 20-foot chestnut canoe—$900 for the whole new outfit. At that time it was really cheap."
David Roland (1992, Tape 53)

It was clear by 1956 that the government's plan to create a reindeer industry consisting of a few privately owned Native herds was not going to work. What were they going to do with the reindeer? If they got rid of them, they would be losing over one million dollars.

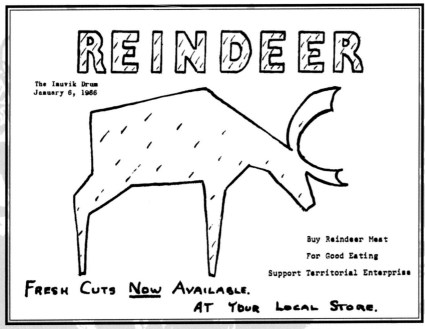

Advertisement for reindeer meat in the newspaper, *Inuvik Drum*, January 6, 1966.[52]

Sven Johansson, 1970. (Dick Hill)

Creating a Commercial Enterprise

Once most of the Native herds quit operating, the government decided to try running the herd as a meat-selling business. This meant hiring herders as employees, who would be paid a salary like other government workers.[53]

In 1960, the government contracted out the management of the herd to John J. Teal, who was the Director of the Institute of Northern Agricultural Research in Vermont. His partner until 1961 was Al Oeming, who ran a game farm in Alberta.[54] Eventually Oeming took over in 1963. He hired Sven Johansson from Sweden to manage the herd. Johansson took over the herd from Oeming two years later and ran it until 1968.[55]

Johansson tried to find ways to operate the herd more efficiently. He switched to open or "extensive" herding. This meant that the reindeer were not constantly herded, but were allowed to roam freely within certain grazing areas. He also established winter ranges for the reindeer near Inuvik. There is more shelter there in the trees, and a richer growth of reindeer moss (lichen).

The animals were rounded up into groups of 2,000 or so, using dog teams in winter and airplanes and boats in summer.[56] Slaughters were carried out at Atkinson Point and Ren Lake, near the route followed by the reindeer.

For open herding, far fewer herders were needed. Under the close herding system, the main herd sometimes had 16 herders for 3,000 reindeer. With open herding, it was thought that only 10 herders were needed to look after 30,000 reindeer. That was the number of reindeer they estimated there would be in ten years.[57] Despite these improvements, there seemed to be a large number of reindeer missing when they were counted, using photos taken from the air, in 1967.[58]

In 1968, the government turned the herd over to the Canadian Wildlife Service (CWS) to manage. The CWS conducted research to develop better management practices and figure out how to make the herd increase in number.[59] Reindeer Station was closed, and the new project was run from Inuvik.

Robert Nowosad became the manager and was successful in increasing the numbers of reindeer by using the open herding method. The reindeer were allowed to find their own way through the grazing grounds, and the winter grazing grounds were rotated. There were only four herders, who did their job using snowmobiles. During this time the government was trying to decide what to do with the herd.

Value of Reindeer Components 1965–66 Winter Wholesale Prices

Carcass	125 lb @ 40¢/lb	$50.00
Head	12 lb @ 10¢	1.20
Legs	4 lb @ 30¢	1.20
Skins		2.00
Antlers	5 lb @ 20¢	1.00
Offal	55 lb @ 2¢	1.10
		Total	$56.50

Above right: Robert Nowosad, 2001. Mr. Nowosad ran the reindeer operation for the Canadian Wildlife Service from 1968 to 1973. (Courtesy of Joanne Nowosad)

Estimated 1967 Population of Primary Market Areas for Reindeer Products

Mackenzie Delta		Slave Lake		Mackenzie River	
Inuvik	3,000	Yellowknife	3,600	Good Hope	350
Aklavik	700	Fort Smith	2,000	Fort Norman	300
Fort McPherson	600	Hay River	2,000	Norman Wells	100
Tuktoyaktuk	500	Resolution	500	Fort Franklin	300
Arctic Red River	100	Fort Rae	600	Wrigley	150
Reindeer Station	100	Discovery	200	Simpson	600
		Providence	400	Other	200
		Other	200		
	5,000		9,500		2,000

Silas Kangegana (herd owner), George Roach (former mayor of Inuvik), Bob Panaktalok (herder), and Dr. Gordon Godkin (government veterinarian). No Date. Photo reversed. (Courtesy of Laura Kangegana)

Inuvialuit Owned!

Silas Kangegana

In 1974, Silas Kangegana purchased the reindeer herd from the government. Silas was a skilled and respected herder. He called his company Canadian Reindeer Company Limited.[60] Silas used fixed-wing aircraft to monitor the locations of the herd and also introduced the use of helicopters.

Silas Kangegana's old corral at Kangilik, McKinley Bay, 1995. (John Poirier)

Inset image: Antlers in velvet. (Based on photo by D. Wilkinson/NWT Archives N-1979-051-1143)

Laura Kangegana. Laura and Silas Kangegana came from Alaska to join the reindeer operation. (John Poirier)

Silas Kangegana and unidentified man. Note the early model snowmobile. (© ISDP/Bessie Wolkie Collection/21)

A new means of income was generated through the sale of antlers in velvet to a Southeast Asian market. Some Southeast Asians think that ground-up antler in velvet has medicinal value. Antlers are said to be "in velvet" when they are first forming in early summer. At that time they consist of blood vessels and tissue that help the antlers form. Silas continued to use the facility at Atkinson Point and also had a corral near the bottom of McKinley Bay. Unfortunately, his health was not good, so he decided to sell the herd.

Silas Kangegana (right) and an unidentified man help Dr. Godkin (left), a government veterinarian, to inspect the reindeer meat. (Courtesy of Laura Kangegana)

William Nasogaluak, Norman Felix and Emmanuel Felix drumming at a drum dance, ca. 1994. (Courtesy of the Inuvialuit Regional Corporation)

William Nasogaluak

In 1978 the herd was sold to William Nasogaluak of Tuktoyaktuk. He called his company Canadian Reindeer (1978) Limited. The reindeer were kept in the Tuktoyaktuk Peninsula area in summer and south of Tuktoyaktuk in the Jonah Lake area in winter. The location of the herd was monitored by fixed-wing aircraft. Snowmobiles were used to move the herd in winter. The Nasogaluaks found that using helicopters was more efficient than having herders on the ground when large numbers of animals needed to be moved in a short period of time. The reindeer used to be harvested for both meat and antler, and live animals were also sold. Later, antler became the sole source of income.

When the Inuvialuit Arctic Claim was settled, some of the reindeer reserve fell within the Inuvialuit Settlement Region. This made the herd subject to new grazing fees. William was involved in litigation with the Department of Indian and Northern Affairs (DIAND), Government of Canada, and the Inuvialuit Regional Corporation for years. He feels that his right to use the reindeer reserve without paying fees was not protected by the government when they negotiated the land claim.

In 1978, William sold 68 reindeer to the Government of the Northwest Territories to send to the Belcher Islands. Most of the caribou there, which were already low in number, had starved after an ice storm created a thick layer of ice over the vegetation they needed for food.

William believes that his family has been important in running the business. He says that his wife Eunice has been steadfast in her support over the years. His brothers Joe and Henry have helped in many ways, and his brother David has been Chief Herder for the last 15 years. Even those of the younger generation have been involved. Among them was William's nephew David Nasogaluak Jr., a commercial pilot, who helped by flying a helicopter to move the herd. David Jr. showed great ability in working with reindeer. Sadly, he died at age 26, while piloting a commercial flight from Banks Island.

David Nasogaluak has been reindeer herding for 22 years, and Chief Herder for 15. (Laura Ettagiak Orchard)

After 22 years in the reindeer business, William is now in the process of selling the herd. The Nasogaluaks want to acknowledge the contribution made by the senior herders who worked with them when they first started the company. Men like Bob Panaktalok, Joseph Avik, Peter Rufus, Adam Emaghok, and Stanley Keevik were not only highly skilled herders, but also teachers: they helped to pass on their knowledge to a younger generation of apprentice herders. To them the Nasogaluaks extend their thanks.

Eunice Nasogaluak, 1997. (Peggy Jay)

Reindeer in the Atkinson Point corral, 1985. (Courtesy of David Nasogaluak)

Looking to the Future

Otto Binder and his reindeer "Monkey." Most sled deers were given names. (Courtesy of Otto Binder)

The Binder Family

At the time this book is being written, the Binder family of Inuvik is in the process of purchasing the reindeer herd. Their company is called Kuññek Resource Development Corporation, with Lloyd N. Binder as General Manager. The senior family members, Otto and Ellen Binder, have a long involvement with the reindeer business. Otto Binder was both a herder and herd manager. Ellen's father Mikkel Pulk, a Saami reindeer herder, was brought to Canada to train local Native people to become herders, and to train and handle sled deer. Ellen was an infant when she arrived with her father and grew up in a life centered around reindeer. Ellen's brother

Nels also provides advice. Given their history and the strong influence of the Pulks' herding culture, it is fitting that some of the younger generation are interested in owning and developing the herd.

The regulatory processes are more complex now than when the herd was last sold. The Binder's application for a grazing lease had to pass an environmental review to ensure that negative impacts to the land and wildlife do not occur. Working relationships must be established with local Inuvialuit organizations and the federal government.

As with most businesses, diversification can be important to economic success. The Binders will continue the harvest of antler. Once the herd size increases, they may resume a harvest for meat. New initiatives include eco-tourism, focusing on the reindeer and the Arctic ecosystem. They may also sell live animals, and embryos and semen for artificial insemination.

Other initiatives may include a system of range management based on the use of remote sensing and Geographical Information Systems (GIS) to track the type and condition of vegetation across the grazing range. A combination of both close and open herding will be used. This may be complemented by the use of satellite or radio collars to keep track of the herd.

Looking Back

The reindeer were brought to the Mackenzie Delta in 1935 to provide a reliable source of meat. Herding was also supposed to provide a way for Inuvialuit to make a living that was more reliable than hunting and trapping. However, the reindeer industry did not turn out exactly as the government had planned. Rather than a number of privately owned Native herds, there is now only one. In the early days of the industry, it was difficult for the government to attract men to herding who wanted to stay with it and become herders or herd owners. Given what we know about the hardships of the herding life, this is not surprising to us now. Although some people enjoyed the herding life, once the DEW Line and other well-paying jobs increased, herding just didn't make financial sense.[61]

Many people feel that the reindeer industry has been a benefit to people in the area. It provided meat and jobs for quite a few people. This was not just for herders, but for handymen and others who worked at Reindeer Station. Many of the herders learned skills and discipline that served them well in future jobs.

> "For the time it existed, it gave a lot of people employment and brought a lot of food to the area. Like I said myself, it wasn't easy when the caribou didn't come and no one had meat to eat. Human-wise, it was a great experience. All the most stable workers in any community are reindeer herders."
>
> **Ellen Binder (1992, Tape 10)**

The elders who stayed with reindeer herding for years remember it as a good experience. They liked the way that people worked together to help each other out. Some found a sense of freedom while being out on the land with the herd. For them, it was more than a job: it was a way of life that they thrived on. Despite the hardships, it was a time they recall with some nostalgia. This is evident in the words used by elder Jimmy Gordon when reflecting on his years as a reindeer herder:

> "That was a very beautiful life, you know. When I think back on it, I miss that life. I really do!"
>
> **Jimmy Gordon (1992, Tape 4)**

Driving part of Charlie Rufus and Rufus Kailialuk's herd toward the corral. Native Herd No. 1, Nicholson Island, N.W.T., August 1943. (Based on photo by A.E. Porsild/National Archives of Canada/PA-101103)

Bibliography

This bibliography includes references cited as well as some relevant articles that were not cited. It also includes titles of published and unpublished reports on or by Inuvialuit that may be of use in the classroom.

Abrahamson, G.
1963   Canada's reindeer. Canadian Geographical Journal 61(6): 189–193.

French, Alice
1976   My Name is Masak. Winnipeg: Peguis Publishers Limited.

Government of Canada
1938   Canada's Reindeer Herd. Ottawa: Lands, Parks and Forests Branch.

Hadwen, I. Seymour
1939   A Visit to the Mackenzie River Delta. Ontario Research Foundation Bulletin 6(12) (December 1939): no page numbers (reprint).

Hart, Elisa J.
1994   Heritage Sites Research, Traditional Knowledge and Training. In: Bridges Across Time: The NOGAP Archaeology Project, edited by Jean-Luc Pilon, Occasional Paper No. 2. Victoria: Canadian Archaeological Association. 15–28.
1995   Getting Started in Oral Traditions Research. Occasional Papers of the Prince of Wales Northern Heritage Centre, No. 4. Yellowknife: Government of the Northwest Territories.
1997   Kitigaaryuit Archaeological Inventory and Mapping Project – 1996. Inuvik: Inuvialuit Social Development Program.
1998   Tuktoyaktuk Traditional Knowledge Project: Sites Listing. Report on file with the Prince of Wales Northern Heritage Centre, Government of the Northwest Territories.
1999   Kitigaaryuit Archaeological Inventory and Mapping Project – 1997. Inuvik: Inuvialuit Social Development Program.

Hart, Elisa J., and Cathy Cockney
1998   Kitigaaryuit: Thoughts on the Impacts of Various Uses of this Important Heritage Site. In: Oakes, J., Riewe, R., Kinew, K. and E. Maloney, eds. Sacred Lands: Aboriginal World Views, Claims, and Conflicts. Occasional Publication No. 43. Edmonton: Canadian Circumpolar Institute. 163–171.
1999   The Yellow Beetle Oral History and Archaeology Project. Inuvik: Inuvialuit Social Development Program.

Hill, Richard M.
1967   Mackenzie Reindeer Operations. Ottawa: Northern Co-ordination and Research Centre, Department of Indian and Northern Development.
1968   The Canadian Reindeer Project. The Polar Record 14(8): 21–24.

Inuvialuit Social Development Program
1991   Inuvialuit Pitqusiit: The culture of the Inuvialuit. Yellowknife: Northwest Territories Department of Education.

Krebs, Charles J.

1961   Population dynamics of the Mackenzie Delta reindeer herd, 1938–1958. Arctic 14(2): 91–100.

Lowe, Ronald

1983   Kangiryuarmiut Uqauhingita Numiktittitdjutingit, Basic Kangiryuarmiut Dictionary. Inuvik: Committee for Original Peoples Entitlement.

1984   Siglit Inuvialuit Uqausiita: Basic Siglit Inuvialuit Eskimo Dictionary. Inuvik: Committee for Original Peoples Entitlement.

1984   Uummarmiut Uqalungiha Mumikhitchirutingit, Basic Uummarmiut Eskimo Dictionary. Inuvik: Committee for Original Peoples Entitlement.

McGhee, Robert

1974   The Beluga Hunters: An archaeological reconstruction of the history and culture of the Mackenzie Delta Kittegaryumiut. Newfoundland Social and Economic Studies No. 13. St. John's: Memorial University of Newfoundland.

Miller, Max

1935   The Great Trek. Garden City: Doubleday, Doran, & Co.

Nagy, Muirelle I.

1994   Yukon North Slope Inuvialuit Oral History. Occasional Papers in Yukon History No.1, Whitehorse: Government of the Yukon.

Nasogaluak, William, and Douglas Billingsley

1981   The reindeer industry in the Western Canadian Arctic. Problems and potential. In: Freeman, M. R. (editor). Proceedings: First International Symposium on Renewable Resources and the Economy of the North. Ottawa: Association of Canadian Universities for Northern Studies. 86–95.

North, Dick

1991   Arctic Exodus: The Last Great Trail Drive. Toronto: Macmillan of Canada.

Nuligak

1966   I, Nuligak. Maurice Metayer (translator). Toronto: Peter Martin and Associates.

Scotter, George W.

1972   Reindeer ranching in Canada. Journal of Range Management 25(3): 167–174.

1978   How Andy Bahr led the great reindeer herd from western Alaska to the Mackenzie Delta. Canadian Geographic 97(2): 12–19.

Seguin, Gilles

1991   Reindeer for the Inuit: The Canadian Reindeer Project, 1929–1960. Muskox 38: 6–26.

Stager, John K.

1984   Reindeer Herding as Private Enterprise in Canada. Polar Record 22(137): 127–126.

Treude, Erhard

1966   The development of reindeer herding in Canada. Geographische Rundschau 49(1): 347–353.

1975   Forty Years of Reindeer Herding in the Mackenzie Delta, N.W.T. Polar Geography 3(3): 121–138.

Usher, Peter
    1971   The Canadian Western Arctic: A century of change. Anthropologica, New Series 13(1): 169–183.

Archival Collections

National Archives of Canada

Accession No.	Collection Name
1973-035	Harry Connor Collection
1973-357	Canada. Indian and Northern Affairs
1974-366	Canada. Indian and Northern Affairs

NWT Archives

Accession No.	Collection Name
G-1979-023	Northwest Territories. Department of Information
G-1979-069	Inter-departmental Reindeer Committee, 1931–1956.
G-1988-012	Sven Johansson, 1987–1988
N-1979-050	Archibald Lang Fleming
N-1979-051	Douglas Wilkinson
N-1979-055	Yellowknife Museum Society
N-1979-062	Terrance Hunt
N-1979-567	Isaac Seymour Hadwen
N-1987-019	Leslie Livingston
N-1987-028	Sven Johansson
N-1987-030	Rex Terpening
N-1990-003	Mary Saich
N-1990-005	Erik Watt
N-1993-002	Robert C. Knights
N-1995-004	The Glenbow-Alberta Institute

Table and Chart Credits

Page 39: Increase in the Main Herd through Fawns: 1935–1940: Based on "Canada's Reindeer." NWT Archives G-1979-069, 1940. p. 3

Page 44: Herd Size from 1935 to 1967: Based on R. M. Hill (1967). pp. 65–67.

Page 44: Composition of the Main Herd in 1940: Based on "Canada's Reindeer." NWT Archives G-1979-069, 1940. p. 3

Page 46: Number of Reindeer for All Herds 1954 Roundups: Based on "Reindeer Project, Northwest Territories." NWT Archives G-1979-069, 1955. p. 4.

Page 51: Number and Use of Slaughtered Reindeer in 1955: Based on "Reindeer Project, Northwest Territories." NWT Archives G-1979-069, 1955. p. 5.

Page 52: Skins Taken In 1955: Based on "Reindeer Project, Northwest Territories." NWT Archives G-1979-069, 1955. p. 5.

Page 86: Buildings at Reindeer Station—1955: Based on "Reindeer Project, Northwest Territories." NWT Archives G-1979-069, 1955. p. 2.

Page 86: Transportation Equipment: Based on "Reindeer Project, Northwest Territories." NWT Archives G-1979-069,1955. p. 2.

Page 97: Value of Reindeer Components 1965–1966 Winter Wholesale Prices: Based on R.M. Hill (1967). p. 136.

Page 97: Estimated 1967 Population of Primary Market Areas for Reindeer Products: Based on R.M. Hill (1967). p. 40.

Films

Canada's Reindeer. 1981. Ottawa: National Film Board of Canada and Inuk Films.

The Herd. 1998. Ottawa: National Film Board of Canada.

Notes

1. The Tuktoyaktuk Traditional Knowledge Project focused on heritage sites research. The goal was to locate places of historical or cultural importance to Inuvialuit in Tuktoyaktuk. This information could be used in impact assessment if oil and gas exploration commenced in the area. The project also involved developing training material for people in communities to undertake this research themselves, or to be co-researchers in interviewing elders. See Hart 1994, 1995, 1998.

2. Seguin, G., 1991, p. 18, says that between 1935 and 1960, about 66 Canadian Inuit worked in the reindeer industry. A report called, "Reindeer Project, Northwest Territories," 1955, says that over 100 received training as staff or assisting at roundup. This is in accession NWT Archives G-1979-069, Inter-departmental Reindeer Committee. Seguin's figure of 66 people may not have included numbers of temporary assistants hired for the roundup.

3. This story of Mangilaluk's resistance to the treaty and his suggestion of bringing reindeer was not recorded in full during our interviews with former reindeer herders. I have summarized the story told to me by Noah Felix, who is the grandson of William Mangilaluk.

4. Personal communication, John Nagy, Caribou/Muskox Biologist, Department of Resources, Wildlife and Economic Development, Government of the Northwest Territories (GNWT), Inuvik Region. See Usher, 1971.

5. Seguin, G., 1991, pp. 7–9, 12. Also D. North, 1991.

6. NWT Archives G-1979-069, report entitled "Canada's Reindeer," dated 1940, p. 1, lists more detail of earlier attempts at reindeer husbandry in Canada. Also from that collection is a report, "Reindeer Herding in Canada," 1956, which describes the government's desire for reindeer herding across the Arctic. See Treude, 1966.

7. North, D., 1991, pp. 8–10.

8. NWT Archives G-1979-069, report entitled "Canada's Reindeer," dated 1940, pp. 1–2.

9. North, D., 1991, p. 58.

10. Ibid., p. 65.

11. I recommend, Arctic Exodus: The Last Great Trail Drive, by Dick North, 1991. An interesting summary is provided by Scotter, 1978.

12. North, D., 1991, p. 160.

13. North, D., 1991, p. 92.

14. The Inuvialuit Social Development Program (ISDP) conducted a survey of the area where the ruins of the old station at Kuururyuaq stand. See Hart (1999). In 1998, ISDP also conducted an oral history and archaeological project related to the RCAF/USAF Loran station at Kuururyuaq. Annie Emaghok talked about the use of the log

cabins when she and her husband were herding in the area. See Hart and Cockney (1999). For more details on the history of Kitigaaryuit, see McGhee (1974) and Hart (1997).

15. NWT Archives G-1979-069, a report entitled "Canada's Reindeer," dated 1940, p. 2.

16. Hart, E., 1997.

17. Treude, E., 1979, p. 123.

18. NWT Archives G-1979-069, report entitled, "Reindeer Project, Northwest Territories," 1955, p. 8, states that 2,382 reindeer were purchased for $154,830.00.

19. NWT Archives G-1979-069, report entitled, "Canada's Reindeer," dated 1940, p. 2.

20. Seguin, G., 1991, p. 10.

21. Ibid. Truede, E., 1979, p. 124.

22. Kidluit Bay on National Topographic Series map 107 C.

23. Plan of reindeer corral is based on Hill, 1967, p. 80. Interesting information on milling is in North, 1991, p. 31.

24. Canada, Department of Mines and Resources, "Canada's Reindeer Herd," 1938, p. 7.

25. NWT Archives G-1979-069, report entitled, "Canada's Reindeer," dated 1940, p. 3.

26. NWT Archives G-1979-069, report entitled, "Reindeer Project, Northwest Territories," 1955, p. 5.

27. Ibid., p. 9.

28. Ibid., p. 5.

29. Ibid., pp. 5–6.

30. Ibid., p. 5.

31. Ibid., p. 14.

32. Hadwen, 1939, no page number, but appears on last page of the article in the section called, "Caribou and Reindeer."

33. There are three dialects of Inuvialuktun. Within the Inuvialuit communities, Siglitun is spoken primarily in Tuktoyaktuk, Sachs Harbour, and Paulatuk. Uummarmiutun is spoken mostly in Aklavik and Inuvik. Kangiryuarmiutun is spoken in Holman Island. The Committee for Original Peoples Entitlement produced a dictionary and grammar for each dialect. The dictionaries are listed in the references under Lowe.

34. Seguin, E., 1991, p. 11.

35. Ibid., p. 12.

36. NWT Archives G-1979-069, "Reindeer Bulletin," dated October 31, 1942, p. 2.

37. Seguin, E., 1991, p. 13.

38. Ibid., pp. 11–14.

39. Ibid., p. 16. Treude, E., 1979, p. 126.

40. Ibid., p. 123. The range was extended in 1952.

41. Seguin, E., 1991, p. 16.

42. Ibid., pp. 16–17.

43. Ibid.

44. Ibid.

45. Ibid., p. 17.

46. Ibid., pp. 12,17.

47. NWT Archives G-1979-069, "Annual Report, Reindeer Station," N.W.T., April 1, 1958 - March 31, 1959, p. 9. Also NWT Archives G-1988-012, a document by Sven Johansson entitled "The Canadian Reindeer Herd." No page numbers.

48. NWT Archives G-1979-069, "Annual Report, Reindeer Station," N.W.T., April 1, 1958 - March 31, 1959, p. 13.

49. National Archives of Canada, Welfare report from teacher at Tuktoyaktuk, N.W.T for month of June, 1950, p. 2.

50. Ibid.

51. Treude, E., 1979, p. 125, Table 1.

52. Hill, R.M., 1967, p. xi.

53. Seguin, G., 1991, p. 18.

54. Ibid. Treude, E., 1979, p. 129.

55. Treude, E., 1979, p. 129. NWT Archives G-1988-012, a document by Sven Johansson entitled "The Canadian Reindeer Herd." No page numbers.

56. NWT Archives G-1988-012, a document by Sven Johansson entitled "The Canadian Reindeer Herd." No page numbers.

57. Hill, R. M., 1968, p. 23.

58. Treude, E., 1979, p. 130.

59. Ibid., p. 131.

60. Ibid., p. 132.

61. Seguin, G., 1991, pp. 16-22. Treude, E. 1979, p. 128. NWT Archives G-1988-012, a document by Sven Johansson entitled "The Canadian Reindeer Herd." No page numbers.

Lena Anikina (standing), Ken Anikina and Elisa Hart look at the remains of Wallace Lucas' corral near Qiniqsiq, 1993. (Charles Komeak)